D0965506

ANATOMY OF THE STATE DEPARTMENT

Anatomy of the

STATE
DEPARTMENT

Smith Simpson

HOUGHTON MIFFLIN COMPANY BOSTON

1967

FIRST PRINTING W

COPYRIGHT © 1967 BY R. SMITH SIMPSON
ALL RIGHTS RESERVED INCLUDING THE RIGHT TO
REPRODUCE THIS BOOK OR PARTS THEREOF IN ANY FORM
LIBRARY OF CONGRESS CATALOG CARD NUMBER: 66-19840
PRINTED IN THE UNITED STATES OF AMERICA

TO

THOSE OFFICERS

OF THE STATE DEPARTMENT

AND THE FOREIGN SERVICE

WHO HAVE DEVOTED THEMSELVES

UNSELFISHLY TO THE DIPLOMATIC

NEEDS OF THE NATION

Acknowledgments

FOR THE DECISION to write this book, and for the material and ideas that have gone into it, I am indebted to many persons. First, to my parents, for their example of independent thinking and for their ideals which made inevitable my own criteria of public service. Second, to my wife, who, sharing these ideals, has willingly made the sacrifices required by my early retirement from the diplomatic establishment to write this book. Throughout these hard days she has been, as ever, a comforting and encouraging spirit.

Although not many of my colleagues in the diplomatic establishment have encouraged me in this exercise, I am really indebted to them all. In my association with them for over twenty years, beginning prior to my entry into the diplomatic establishment, when none of us knew a book would be written, they all contributed their thinking, experiences, and ambitions; their cooperation and competition; their values and variances. Since they *are* the State Department, I could not have written about it without their insight. Much of what I say here in criticism is said privately by them. I have only added an analysis which I hope may direct this criticism to constructive ends.

I acknowledge the gracious permission of copyright owners to reproduce certain material, and I am grateful to the staff of Houghton Mifflin Company, which has extended me a generosity of professional assistance beyond any I could have reasonably expected.

SMITH SIMPSON

Preface

"ALL HUMAN KNOWLEDGE," said Plato, "begins with *why*."

Many criticisms of the State Department have failed to begin with *why*. They have dealt with symptoms rather than causes and have contributed very little to either insight or reform. This has also been true of many of the reports by Presidential and other commissions appointed to recommend improvements in the Department. It is time someone began with *why*.

Dissatisfaction exists both inside and outside the Department. All too often outside discontent exhausts itself in uninformed excoriation. Criticism from within the Department is more knowledgeable but still not very profound. It is inclined to go off on personal or trivial tangents. Too few insiders have the courage to raise basic issues. Of those who do, too few have the time to pursue them. Of those who do pursue them, too few have the final determination to put them down in cold print.

Many of the causes of dissatisfaction have roots deep in the past. They do not yield to daily tinkering and tampering, yet that is about all they have received over the years. It is time for something more, something I can only hope this book may provide. If, in any case, what I say helps clarify the thoughts of those of us who are concerned, it will have justified the personal pain I have experienced in seeing it through and the greater pain I shall experience from publication.

For this has been a difficult book to write. There is much here that will appear to cast aspersions upon old friends and colleagues in the diplomatic establishment. My only justification is the need of the nation, which must be placed above personal feelings. Had the Department been more hospitable to change from within, this book would not have been needed. I have made a great effort to be as accurate in fact and as fair in judgment as possible.

I trust the reader will be alert to the objective of this study, which is suggested by its title, and will not rashly conclude the State Department does nothing well and has no competent officials. It does some things well and has some able people in it. At the same time, it misuses, even abuses, its most competent officers. It has a way of devouring and dissipating their resources.

This is a diagnosis of obvious symptoms of weaknesses. It is not a general appraisal of what the Department does well as compared with what it does ill.

I trust, also, that the reader will carefully note that I am analyzing the Department and its officers from the standpoint of organizational and procedural, intellectual, cultural and ethical factors. I do not call in question officers' physical courage and stamina. The bravery of the Michael Hoyts and John Clingermans in the Congo, of the officers in the new Vietnam village program, of the Temple Wanamakers who do not flinch from assassination threats and attempts, and of comparable officers over the years does not present the issues I discuss nor can it answer the questions I raise.

Contents

ANATOMY OF THE
STATE DEPARTMENT

Diplomacy Went Thataway

ALMOST FROM the beginning of our Republic to the eve of World War II, our nation sought to avoid profound entanglements in diplomacy. As colonies, we had had some useful experience with it and had scored creditable successes including, indeed, the winning of our independence. But the rivalries of the Great Powers of Europe threatened to carry us into unfamiliar currents and involve us in situations we considered unnecessarily risky. In addition, we found highly repugnant the bribery and boudoir intriguing that passed for diplomacy.

President Washington's parting injunction to avoid entangling alliances expressed this attitude, and subsequent experience reinforced it. The maneuvers of diplomacy appeared increasingly hazardous, and they rarely seemed to yield what we wanted. Even when, by some miracle, European power politics brought us success, our negotiators emerged humiliated. The purchase of Louisiana is an example: the negotiations which won for us that immense territory also forced our government to assume debts owed to American citizens by

France, leading to a scandal that blackened the reputation of one negotiator and jeopardized the public career of the other. With success bought on such harsh terms, diplomacy appeared singularly unattractive.

Moreover, purchase of the vast Louisiana territory gave us a continent to develop. As the nation turned to the settlement of its domain beyond the Appalachian passes, it was not insulated from the necessity of negotiation with foreign powers. From the beginning of colonization, of course, settlement had involved negotiation — negotiation with British authorities and subsequently with French, Spanish and Mexican, as well as with Indian nations. But as this negotiation continued during the westward migration, it came to be regarded as negotiation close to home, concerned only with our own continental development. It was not viewed as entangling us in the affairs of others.

Our relations with the rest of the world came more and more to be those of an aloof spectator. Observation, not action; reportage, not maneuver; the following of day-to-day events, not the mapping of large strategy and tactics, came to typify our stance overseas. Our diplomatic representatives were generally expected to remain on the sidelines, keeping Washington informed but avoiding a tricky business at which others were considered more adept and which others seemed to need more than we. It was thus that our diplomats came to be officially described as "the eyes and ears of our Government abroad." Their tools were little more than a pair of eyes, a pair of ears and a quill.

There were exceptions. A particularly cultivated merchant, like Townsend Harris, could open up Japan to economic and political intercourse. A professional in international law, like Henry Wheaton, could bargain hard and well over seizures of American ships, gaining not only recognition of our rights and compensation for wrongs, but respect and standing for himself and the nation as well. A broadly educated practitioner of the law and an eloquent speaker, such as Joseph H. Choate, might, as ambassador, use the many speaking occasions given him to educate his overseas audiences in American history, democratic principles, processes and institutions. But by and large the reporting tradition became deeply entrenched, and it persists even today. Most old-time diplomatic officers will tell you that their primary function is to report, and they can point to all sorts of State Department publications to prove it.

Furthermore, over the years the foreign service developed a debilitating fraternity spirit. This, too, had roots in a general phenomenon of our history. From the administration of the first frontiersman President, Andrew Jackson, our suspicions of diplomacy received hearty endorsement. Frontiersmen denigrated the diplomatic process as mere talk, mere fancy-pants stuff, and they insisted that they wanted action, and plenty of it, with all the lace and frills aside. In such an atmosphere, diplomacy other than the homespun sort came to be considered unfit for virile men. This attitude even manifested itself in cultured seaboard circles, where a sober, industrious, well-educated father in the 1890s could be horrified to discover that his son was interested in a diplomatic career, which to the practical father was "parasitical." A leading congressman from the Middle West, who became a serious contender for his party's nomination for President in 1912, went so far as to advocate the abolition of our diplomatic service.

Diplomacy, little understood, was considered at best a pursuit for social butterflies, and at worst a kind of social disease sapping the vitals of a vigorous, enterprising, independent democracy.

Our diplomatic service thus evolved in a prevalently hostile atmosphere until very recent times and was largely confined to recruits from the Eastern seaboard, as a result of which it became the object of a redoubled suspicion based on regional sensibilities in the extensive Middle and Far West.

Upon its devotees, however, diplomacy cast a very real spell. It offered the glittering society of the illustrious as well as hazard and adventure. It provided cultural opportunities not available at home. Such attractions, coupled with the ridicule of outsiders, generated a fraternal bond among those who ventured to pursue the calling. For its members, the diplomatic service came to be a kind of mystic order whose secrets they alone knew, and into which bumbling ignoramuses, like Midwestern Congressmen, as well as stay-at-home civil servants in the State Department and the diplomats' consular colleagues, not to add academic specialists in foreign policy and diplomacy, could hardly expect to be initiated.

This fraternal spirit engendered a disdain for "outsiders" and their criticism that led to smugness. This, in turn, generated resistance to reform. Times might change, but not the devotees of diplomacy and their habits of mind. They had to be clubbed over the head before they would accept merger with the collateral consular corps, which, operating in foreign cities and towns outside the glittering capitals, and without the benefit of diplomatic immunities and privileges, did just about everything the diplomatic corps did except negotiate treaties and deal with national ministries. Merger of the two corps, finally achieved in 1924 as the result of Congressional action, did not destroy the diplomatic fraternity however. On the contrary, the fraternity stiffened, preempting positions of control within the merged services and assuring its members preferred assignments and the lion's share of promotions. So unconscionably was this favoritism practiced that a vigilant Congress finally intervened and insisted on more equitable conduct.

The fraternity similarly resisted the lessons of the worldwide depression of 1929 and of World War II. These events, bringing into the diplomatic establishment a flood of new personnel with unconventional ideas and skills, were met with as much comprehension as the Revolution of 1789 by the French nobility. The world was in fact registering a revolution, but the heedless fraternity bided its time, treating the new officers as fugitive competitors brought to surface by a transient emergency. All the postwar pressures to retain the progressive, versatile newcomers were resisted. Even when Congress enacted a law to provide for the newcomers' retention, the fraternity voted in only a small number of them. Those working in the information and cultural programs became so frustrated that in desperation they sought outlet in an autonomous agency. So, too, a separate agency had to be established for the Marshall Plan, and subsequent technical assistance had to be administered wholly outside the State Department. When merger of the Department's domestic civil service staff with the Foreign Service was proposed, it too was resisted, and only when John Foster Dulles arrived on the scene was the opposition overcome.

A fraternal hiss accompanied the civil servants into the diplomatic service. These officials had spent years working on foreign affairs, albeit from behind desks in Washington. They lacked many qualities needed to operate successfully abroad, but they were not novices and had a substantial contribution to make. Nevertheless, instead of being encouraged they were treated as interlopers, until, unable to cope with widespread hostility, many gradually resigned or were "selected out," and the Department was obliged to replace them with greenhorns recruited in a labor market more competitive than ever before.

There are men who, in Henry Adams' phrase, grow up in the "habit of looking at life as a social relation — an affair of society." This attitude in fact can be one of the strong impulses propelling men to pursue a diplomatic career. An American has described the scene which attracted him to the calling in this way: "The light from the great chandeliers flashed on the diamond tiaras of the women. Enormous jewels winked from the turbans of Indian princes, clad in red, blue and yellow silks, and draped in ropes of pearls. I had never seen such dazzling attire . . . I went back to the hotel that night so wrought up that for hours I could not sleep. No matter how successful I might be at the law, I was certain I could not possibly find it so exciting as diplomacy." This love of the glitter of society and of the special treatment diplomatic status provides runs through the establishment, exercising a subtle, snobbish influence upon its whole idea of diplomacy and interfering with the effective utilization of the nation's resources in conducting its foreign relations.

There can be no bitterer competition, however, than among

socialites. There are no keener, less conscionable warriors than those fighting for position and status. However closely knit a fraternal organization the diplomatic service came to be vis-à-vis outsiders, *within* the circle members remained zealous, sometimes savage competitors for promotion and the social position that goes with it. There came to exist — and still exists — an exaggerated competitiveness undermining ethical standards and concern for the national interest. This has accentuated a prima-donna approach to diplomacy and too often subjected the formulation of policies and their execution to an excessive pressure of private ambitions, scramblings for assignments, maneuvers for promotion, and other personal considerations.

Perhaps it was natural that, during the years following 1829, when suspicion of diplomacy became a formalized national attitude, those who elected to become diplomats should do so for strongly personal reasons: to gratify a desire for travel, to quench a thirst for adventure, to study languages and cultures, to participate in the glitter of high society, to gain a prestige which intrinsic ability or conditions at home denied. While some of our officers over the years have been serious, dedicated, professionally prepared people, other officers (and their wives) have had so extraordinary an appetite for promotion as to almost invariably covet ambassadorial rank. This desire for the top led to an overdeveloped sense of status, minimized the sober business of policy making, research, planning, management and diplomacy itself. It developed self-promotion to a finished art, forcing officers to pay more attention to their personal security than to the nation's. These factors have sapped a good deal of reality from the law passed forty years ago to screen the diplomatic establishment from external political influence. Politicking from without has been replaced by intensified politicking within.

A few years ago, the Department succeeded in aggravating internal rivalry by adopting an "up-or-out" rule. This highly questionable criterion of good performance, demanding that officers get promoted or retire, is all the more dubious since promotion often occurs from maneuver, ingratiation and chance rather than from equitably enforced professional criteria. It has become all the more open to skepticism by encouraging conformity. There has always been a high degree of the yes-man spirit in our diplomatic establishment. The up-or-out rule has enhanced it.

The hypersensitivity to criticism induced by fraternalism, conformity and a sense of isolation has been noticeable even in many of the more effective career officers. One of them remarked in his later years, not so long ago:

> The healthy fact that there are criticisms from time to time does not bother me as it once did. I remember, for example, that I returned to Washington from North Africa back in 1943 with a very high temperature generated by some critical editorials and stories which had appeared in the *Washington Post* concerning the policies we were then pursuing in that area. I could hardly wait to get off the airplane to visit Mr. Eugene Meyer [publisher of the *Post*]. I had selected *a priori* some very purple words to express my indignation over the obtuseness and general myopia of the author, and I asked to meet the guy who wrote the items. In retrospect it no doubt was a silly performance. Mr. Meyer was indulgent and mildly suggested that in public life one must learn to take it. Then he suggested lunch with the author, Herbert Elliston, to whom he introduced me. After lunch we exchanged some rather

sharp words, but I learned that the items were based on information which Elliston believed sound and accurate. He was kind enough to listen to my version and later to reflect some of it in subsequent articles.

This maturity is not always reached. When it is, as in this case, it comes late in an officer's career, during the greater part of which he has been excessively bothered by suggestions of better policies and performance, and has joined with his colleagues in attributing criticism from without to obtuseness and general myopia and criticism from within to unspeakable treachery. So keenly resented has criticism been over the years that its points have been rarely deemed worthy of serious consideration and its factual validity has been generally dismissed disdainfully without examination.

For all its pretensions to possessing an elite corps of diplomatic officers, State has never succeeded in developing a permanent corps generally capable of really profound interest in the basic tasks of foreign policy and diplomacy. That corps, as a corps, has never appreciated the vast national resources outside itself. It has therefore never acquired the depth of learning demanded by our role of leadership in world affairs.

The impact of all this upon criteria for admission to the diplomatic establishment has been enormous. The State Department and Foreign Service are concerned with foreign policy and diplomacy. They claim a professional interest in these things. They must possess a deeply professional competence in them. One would conclude, therefore, that for admission they would require of candidates a thorough, not to say profound, knowledge of foreign policy, diplomacy, international organization and international law. They don't.

Before one can be admitted to the practice of a profession

such as law, one must have capped a liberal arts preparation with three years in a law school and one must show, by a bar examination, a grasp of the substance and procedures of jurisprudence. In the case of medicine, the requirements are even stiffer, since human life is involved — four years in medical school on top of general college work and a concluding internship in which further searching examinations of knowledge and capability are made. Diplomacy and foreign policy, like the law, involve justice and order. Like medicine, they involve people's lives, and on a very large scale. Successes and failures can affect the life and fortune of every citizen. Diplomacy, therefore, should demand the most thorough, the most grueling professional preparation. Yet the State Department moseys along, requiring no more than was required fifty or sixty years ago. It takes the position that any adult, aged twenty-one, can make a good diplomatic officer if he has but personality, character, a high IQ and a smattering of a liberal arts education.

The simplicity of this notion in a complex world is extraordinary. It is equivalent to holding that anyone with these simple qualifications can make a good lawyer, a good doctor, a good engineer. Of course he can, if he *also* possesses the thorough knowledge, aptitudes and training demanded by the complexities of his calling. Unlike any other profession, however, that of foreign affairs is deemed by the Department to require *no* preparation, save of the most superficial sort.

Although our diplomatic officers must represent the United States, relatively few know anything extensive and solid about their country. They are the ones who must practice diplomacy, but few know what it is except in a superficial way. They must uphold international law but do not know its principles, processes or possibilities. They must operate and coordinate our alliances and our part in the many international organizations to which we belong, but receive their commissions knowing little or nothing of them. They form the front-line battalions of democratic defense but, beyond a few clichés, many cannot discuss intelligently what democracy is, what its principles are, what its techniques and problems are, what it offers that communism cannot.

What does the Department do to correct these catastrophic deficiencies? Very little. Newly commissioned officers are not thrown into a grueling one-, two-, or three-year training to get them set for their profession. They are given only a six-week orientation course, just recently reduced from eight weeks, with an added four weeks a few years later. Moreover, the quality of the initial orientation, while appreciably improved in recent years, is still at a high-school-senior level. No examinations are given during these periods to determine how much of the course the novitiates absorb. A more casual approach to the hard overseas tasks of the nation could scarcely be conceived.

Following this superficial introduction to foreign policy and diplomacy, the newly commissioned officers spend two (recently reduced from four) weeks on technical consular duties, four to six months learning a foreign language, and three weeks acquiring a slight familiarity with the geographic areas to which they will be sent on their first overseas assignments. Their entire indoctrination lasts between seven and nine months, the greater part of which is devoted to gaining varying degrees of linguistic competence.

Thereafter, some years later, if an officer has exceptionally good fortune, he may get a one-week course on some area to which he may be assigned, or a course on the current American scene, or a two-week exposure to talks on communist strategy. If extremely fortunate, he has heretofore had a chance in mid-career to spend twelve weeks superficially reviewing material in which he should have had thorough training at the outset, and which he should already have used diligently in his various assignments. At present, the twelve-week brush-up is being abandoned in favor of one-week courses on various subjects, which the mid-career officer is required to sandwich into a full-time job in the Department. Only a few of these, therefore, is he likely to get. A senior officer, some ten years before retirement, has a very slight chance to get to a seminar of ten months, again receiving instruction he should have had at the beginning of his career.

The Kennedy Administration challenged this laxness. The Department was pressured into adding a course on counter-insurgency against Communism abroad. This was in 1962, seventeen years after the end of World War II had brought the threat of communist attack to the doorstep of our diplomatic establishment. Late in coming though it was, it could have become a valuable course, if given to every officer at the outset of his career and repeated in increasing doses. The course, however, is limited to a few officers and is a one-shot inoculation. Furthermore, like so much else in the Department, it began negatively, emphasizing countering the Communists rather than promotion of positive steps to freedom and democracy.

Admittedly, intellectual preparation and development are only two factors in successful foreign policy and diplomacy. Political instinct and experience also count, for diplomacy is foreign policy in action. Diplomacy is politics. As Dean Acheson has put it, "one should take care not to bank too heavily on the saving power of mere intellectual improvement up and down the line. Not knowledge alone, but how it is marshaled by will and brought to bear in action, must remain the determining consideration in the conduct of foreign policy. Intellectual capabilities . . . are not to be scorned. Indeed, they are to be valued and cultivated, for they can contribute appreciably to the making of sound and effective policy . . . the critical and central considerations must remain, however, the factors of insight and will . . ."

For these factors, however, the Department has only a dilettante's concern. No political experience whatever is required for admission to the diplomatic establishment and no tests have been developed of candidates' political judgment. Various *symptoms* of political instinct are indeed demanded — such things as tact, sense of humor, ingratiating manners — but more because they are the qualities the fraternity likes to find in its brothers, than because they are indicators of a politically oriented mind.

With political experience and instinct at a minimal level in the diplomatic establishment, it is not surprising that the tradition of merely observing, reporting and doing the day's work has persisted and that imaginative diplomatic operators have continued to be scarce in the Department. The cardinal rules of conduct have come to be, not profound study, imaginative strategic planning, and dynamic political action to maintain the nation's initiative abroad, but "keep your mouth shut and your nose clean." It is scarcely any wonder that effective diplomacy has so largely deserted our diplomatic establishment.

CHAPTER 2

Who Runs
the State Department?

IT USED TO BE TRUE, as President Coolidge once said, that "The Secretary of State *is* the Department of State" and whether the Department operates "efficiently or loosely, vigorously or mildly, wisely or shortsightedly," depends primarily upon its chief. Today, however, the Secretary of State is far from being the Department of State. World affairs have developed beyond the reach of a single man, however capable, and a Secretary would only court disaster by acting as though they had not.

Another change in the Secretary's status has occurred. Once primarily the manager of an executive department, he served as adviser on foreign affairs only when the President so desired, which was not invariably the case. Indeed, it was not unknown for a Secretary of State to be appointed on the understanding that he would leave foreign affairs decisions to the President and simply look after his departmental chores. Rarely was he involved in matters crucial to the survival of the nation.

All this has changed. The Secretary of State is obliged daily to cope with forces directed against the nation's security. He has therefore become inevitably a close associate and adviser of the President and the Secretary of Defense. Events have welded these three men into a kind of modern Atlas, to bear upon their shoulders an awesome weight of worldwide responsibilities.

The Secretary's role of manager has thus acquired a broad governmental base. Because of this, his office has unprecedented responsibilities toward other executive departments of the government. Interests in foreign affairs permeate the executive branch, and its resources for effective contribution to international relationships have increased. So intertwined have domestic and foreign affairs become that virtually every part of the Executive establishment is involved in overseas responsibilities. Even the Department of Interior is no longer strictly interior. Every Cabinet member, accordingly, feels he can legitimately advise the President on foreign affairs and each considers himself better informed on some of those affairs than the Secretary of State.

The Secretary's relations with Congress have also changed, because the interest of Capitol Hill in foreign affairs has intensified. Theoretically, the legislative branch is distinct from the executive, and the Secretary of State is supposed to operate as an adviser and agent of the President alone. But the necessities of foreign policy and diplomacy allow few distinctions between executive and legislative interests. Congress is not only involved in appropriations and other legislation required to give effect to State Department efforts, but also in investigating and passing judgment on those efforts both as an incident to its legislating function and as an expression of concern for the national security. As elected representatives of the nation's citizenry congressmen demand more and more information, insisting that the Secretary spend more and more of his time on Capitol Hill, analyzing and explaining the government's policies and diplomatic moves.

In congressional relationships, as in Cabinet, the head of the diplomatic establishment is hard put to maintain a satisfactory equilibrium between foreign and domestic affairs. Congressional action on a supposedly domestic matter can offend an ally. It may run counter to our position in an international organization. It may even violate a treaty or adversely affect a whole system of international security. It may give comfort to an enemy. Somehow, the Secretary and his associates must reconcile these conflicts and forestall as many of them as possible.

Such problems do not occur only when Congress acts as a body. They can arise from the actions of an individual member, if he is influential at home and well-known abroad. A single legislator can nullify a policy studiously investigated and laboriously worked out by the State Department, or thoroughly humiliate its head, as when the great Borah of Idaho arrogantly asserted on July 18, 1939, at a White House conference, that there would be no European war in the near future. So certain was he of this, claiming sources of information superior to the State Department's, that he reduced the Secretary of State to bewildered silence. "Tears actually came to Hull's eyes," says one account of the meeting, "and when the discussion began again and someone asked his opinion, he said bitterly that he had nothing further to offer in view of Borah's remark."

The confusions of debate in Washington over foreign policy can have devastating impact abroad. If some ridiculous or indiscreet statement is made in a committee or on the floor of Congress, it can soar to the furthermost corners of the earth, wreaking havoc everywhere. In its explosive course, it can arouse long-dormant passions, raise doubts, create new questions, revive old ones, reinforce prejudices, until sometimes a weary Secretary of State and his associates hardly know where or how to begin grappling with its effects.

This has heightened the importance of the Secretary's role as head of the Federal diplomatic establishment. He is a hub around which revolve foreign ambassadors resident in Washington and visiting ministers of foreign affairs. Their numbers are larger than ever before; the questions that perplex them are greater. He must remove the blurring effects of Congressional disputation. The Secretary's relations with the diplomatic corps have therefore come to constitute a crucial factor in our efforts to translate foreign policy decisions into desired results.

Great as these responsibilities are, they are not the only ones. The Secretary's presence is often demanded abroad. Not only must the confused clatter of an open society's discussion of its foreign affairs be clarified, but the manner in which such clarification is to be made has become important. The mere presence or absence of the Secretary in a discussion abroad is a kind of noiseless noise indicating our current position with respect to some issue, some arrangement, or some objective scheduled for reevaluation. Psychological factors, as well as world developments, therefore demand of the Secretary a good deal of overseas travel. He has become a migratory definer of policy, silencer of doubt, reassurer, persuader to action.

The Secretary, finally, has an important responsibility to the

American public. He is obliged to take particular pains to keep informed not only the people's representatives in Washington but the people themselves. More individual interests than ever are at stake in foreign affairs. So are the collective interests of a democratic society fighting for survival. National morale, on which our whole defense depends, must be maintained, and this cannot be left solely to the President. Nor can a Secretary ever forget that foreign affairs have become pivotal campaign issues.

All this is clear enough and generally understood, but one important implication is not. So extensive and exacting are these roles that they leave the head of the State Department little or no time to give to his own organization. To the degree that he plays well these roles outside the Department, he becomes a third President, second only to the Vice President. To the extent that he becomes a third President, his role as department manager evaporates. Indeed, the Secretary has been compelled to delegate or relinquish so much to subordinate officials that, individually or collectively, they have become little Secretaries of State.

One of these subordinates, the Under Secretary, is the second-in-command. Others are Deputy Under Secretaries. Beneath them are Assistant Secretaries, one for each principal division of the world's landmass — Europe, Latin America, the Far East, the Near East and South Asia, and Africa — and others for such activities as economic and cultural affairs, intelligence, research and planning, and relations with Congress and international organizations.

The Department thus consists of a broad, pyramidal structure of geographic and functional bureaus headed by the Assistant Secretaries. The geographic bureaus have in the past borne the brunt of the Department's work of digesting information and making daily decisions, and they still consider themselves the custodians of the Republic's real diplomacy. Recent economic, cultural, military and other factors have, however, lessened the significance of national and even continental boundaries and as a result the Department has been trying for some years to bring functional offices into greater play. This has been difficult to do, because the geographic bureaus have been staffed largely by diplomatic officers, while the functional, by civil servants. The attempt to bridge the rift between the two by attaching to geographic bureaus advisers on such subjects as economic and public affairs and politico-military matters has been only moderately successful. The assignment of diplomatic officers to the functional bureaus has been ameliorative. But the jealousy of the geopraphic bureaus over their traditional power has made their integration with the functional bureaus extremely difficult.

At the bottom of the pyramid has traditionally sat the "country desk officer." There was at least one such officer assigned to cover each country in the world. It was his responsibility to follow affairs in the nation of his concern, digest incoming dispatches and telegrams, riffle through as much other pertinent information as the hours of his day permitted, and suggest what the United States should do on a daily or weekly basis with respect to that country. He was so buried in telegrams and dispatches and so preoccupied with routine matters that only with difficulty could he rouse himself for proposals of imaginative or long-range action. Moreover, a junior officer, he was dependent for advancement on the amiable disposition

of the officers above him, who wrote evaluations of his personality, character and performance known as "efficiency reports." What with the clatter of routine business and the pressure of conformity, he too seldom detected matters of real importance and alerted his superiors to them.

The country desk officer gradually receded in importance in
our foreign relations generally. Too many other departments
and agencies of our government came to have similar officers.
Outside government, a variety of business, labor and religious
organizations acquired comparable operators. Educational
and philanthropic institutions have country specialists who are
less harried and more thorough than the State Department's
desk man. In fact, the latter came to be but one element in a
vast complex of public and private relationships sustained by
our nation with every other part of the world.

But the desk officer remained of crucial importance to the
operations of State itself. He could catalyze action if he had
the knowledge, imagination, motivation and courage to do so.
He could help tie the Department together by systematic,
imaginative consultation with his opposite numbers in other
bureaus. He could do the same for the entire Federal establishment. On the other hand, he could reduce his Government's performance to superficial, prosaic terms if he lacked
these qualities, or dwelt too much upon his personal advancement. In fact, the deficiencies of most desk officers were so
great as to generate proposals to put more senior officers, even
ambassadors, into his job. Secretary Rusk has been one of
those thinking along this line.

In March of last year, when, on the advice of General Maxwell Taylor, the President intervened to remind the Depart-

ment of some of its important responsibilities, Rusk took the occasion to order a revamping of the Department's lower level of organization. He superseded the "desk officer" of junior rank with a "country director" of senior grade. Two layers of officers — office directors and deputy office directors — between the "desk officers" and the Assistant Secretaries have been abolished. Theoretically, therefore, Assistant Secretaries will be directly accessible to the "country directors." Actually, since this access will place so heavy a load upon the Assistant Secretaries — already hard pressed — more Deputy Assistant Secretaries will probably have to be appointed to share the burden. If so, the latter will, in effect, take the place of the now-abolished office directors, in which event, one layer — not two layers — of authority will have been eliminated. Whatever may happen in this respect, there is hope that the existence of senior officers at the bottom of the pyramid will introduce greater initiative on the more important matters. But as Secretary Rusk has repeatedly said, "No organizational chart can substitute for the abilities and attitudes of people."

In this large, sprawling, pyramidal structure we perceive one of the cruelest dilemmas of the Secretary and one of the principal blocks to the efficient operation of the Department. The roles the Secretary must play outside the Department are so important that he cannot neglect them, yet they consume so much of his time that he cannot adequately manage the vast pyramid on which depend his success — and the nation's. His role as an adviser to the President, to his Cabinet colleagues, to Congress and to the public requires that he be able to draw rapidly to himself the best information and insights of his department, including those of the lowest level. His role as an executor of foreign policy demands that he be able to assure a prompt, thorough, imaginative follow-through of decisions. But all this depends in turn upon the attitudes, staffing, procedures and other organizational arrangements, not to add mechanical equipment, of the huge bureaucracy over which he presides and from which he must get that very information, insight and action.

The Secretary must not only mobilize the experience and resources of able subordinates. He must also assure that experience and resources are not eroded by unfavorable procedures and criteria of performance. He must assure that attitudes prejudicial to initiative and boldness are adequately challenged. He must overcome established lethargies, provincialisms, premises which lag behind the facts of world developments. He must assure that officers' minds are constantly stimulated, their perspectives broadened and their insights deepened. In all this he dare not neglect what might appear a humdrum matter, like staffing. Overstaffed offices, sluggish in response to his efforts, must be trimmed; understaffed offices, inconducive to clearheaded, penetrating thinking, must be expanded.

Most important, a Secretary must provide his associates — and indeed the Federal community and our allies — with a basic strategy and plan of action. Sooner or later he learns that he is the conductor of a vast departmental orchestra, with many musicians, his baton invisible to all save a limited number, any one of whom can spoil the desired effect. He also discovers that he is trying to lead this orchestra without benefit of a score. Each bureau, each office within a bureau, to some extent each officer beneath him, is improvising from day to day, all too unaware of other bureaus and all too unprepared to play the proper part. This situation — also true of the Federal Government as a whole — explains why Secretaries find it is one thing to inform and advise and another thing to *do* — to function promptly, concertedly, with all the various instruments which a World Power must use. Precisely here does management play a decisive role in all that the Secretary — and the nation — are trying to do in foreign affairs.

Two Secretaries have understood this fact and seriously applied themselves to the role of departmental management. General George C. Marshall was accustomed to command, having had extensive overseas and diplomatic experience as well as having directed a large organization in the military establishment. As a manager in the area of foreign affairs, he knew his way around. His successor, Dean Acheson, had studied the State Department thoroughly as a member of the Hoover Commission for government reorganization (1947), and had served six years in the State Department, first as an Assistant Secretary (1941–45) and then, under Marshall, as Undersecretary (1945–47). He, too, knew his way around.

Appalled by the inefficiency of the Department and its well-nigh total absorption in daily improvisation, Marshall revitalized an executive secretariat as a managerial instrument. This group, attached to his office, followed up on every decision he made and he gave it considerable authority. He also created a planning staff. Systematic study and thinking, planning and follow-through were thus brought into the establishment on a broad scale for the first time. Furthermore, with the establishment of the Foreign Service Institute in 1947, a more adequate instrument for the training of officers was provided. In addition, the War Manpower Act of the year before made possible an infusion of greater versatility of skills and talent into the entire diplomatic establishment.

Unfortunately, the genius of Marshall and his successor was not shared either by the Department's pyramidal mass nor by John Foster Dulles. Under Marshall and Acheson, the planning staff got deeply involved both in current international situations and in long-range problems like the relationship of our military power to our diplomacy. While performing brilliantly in these areas, the planning staff had far to go in others, particularly in the area of developing the basic score so desperately needed by the whole foreign affairs orchestra of the Federal Government. Even what it did outline it had difficulty communicating to the pyramidal mass, which ridiculed and resisted the planning concept. The planning staff's great efforts to think ahead tapered off under Dulles, who, like most career officers, was highly individualistic and an improviser par excellence. He gave the planners a deluge of daily chores, including the drafting of speeches, and drew upon their director for assistance on so many immediate problems, entailing such prolonged absences abroad, that the painstaking business of basic planning atrophied. So did much of the efficient follow-through work of the executive secretariat. Training became pedestrian. Unable to manage his establishment adequately and lacking firm political guidance from the President in the McCarthy controversy, Dulles yielded ground to the Wisconsin Senator's attacks. On top of all this came Dulles's imperial order to merge the civil servants of the Department with the Foreign Service. Morale plummeted.

The management of a diplomatic establishment is a tall

order. It consists of far more than mere administrative supervision. It includes leadership in the development of policy and diplomacy in all their intricate requirements through a careful selection of the best possible personnel, the development of skills, and a unison of effort throughout the diplomatic establishment, in Washington and abroad. It involves developing among all officers — not just a few — a deep understanding of the myriad political, economic, legal, cultural and other factors which affect national survival and world leadership. It means introducing into the Department all the up-to-date techniques of the behavioral sciences for this purpose. It means developing a basic score by which the entire diplomatic establishment can concert its resources and those of our allies as well. It means providing that push of imaginative thinking and follow-through which spells the difference between active leadership and mere response to the moves and policies of other governments. Finally, it means assuring conditions of service which can bring to fruit all efforts along these lines.

If no Secretary save two has assumed this role because of the pressure of other responsibilities and other limitations, can it be delegated? Who does the Secretary have available for such delegation? The next in command, the Under Secretary? This official is ordinarily not selected by the Secretary but chosen by the President. Like the Secretary, he comes from outside the diplomatic establishment, and thus may have scant knowledge of either it or foreign affairs in general. His strong points are not necessarily those a Secretary most requires to complement his own deficiencies and do not necessarily include managerial competence. Like the Secretary, he has rarely managed a large organization. Although he may have native managerial genius, his limited knowledge and experience in the State Department generally deny him the capabilities such a role demands.

The personal relations of the two top officials can also impose serious limitations on the Secretary's delegation of management to this immediate subordinate. Much depends on the temperament and character of the men themselves. If the potential *alter ego* lacks compatibility with the Secretary, or does not earn his respect, he can experience the difficulty of a recent holder of the position who, as one of his intimates put it, had trouble even "finding out the time of day" from his superior.

An Under Secretary may not even wish to accept the status of the Secretary's alternate. One of them recently conceived of his role as that of a catalyst: to stimulate ambassadors and their staffs to a more dynamic diplomacy. As he was often absent from Washington on this self-appointed mission, it would have been impossible to entrust him with the overall management of the establishment.

In addition, coming from the outside, a politically appointed Under Secretary may not stay long. Two years sometimes exhaust his desire to contribute to this particular public service. This, of course, is highly disruptive of delegation even when it might occur for other reasons.

But the greatest frustration is reached on the rare occasions when such limitations are absent and an Under Secretary is still unable to serve as an effective manager. For the abler an Under Secretary is, and the more compatible he is with his chief, the more he must serve as an *alter ego* in substantive matters rather than in management. If the Secretary is unexpectedly summoned to the White House when scheduled to appear before a Congressional committee, such an *alter ego* is ready to take his place with the briefest of briefings, perhaps no more than can be conducted in a taxicab en route. If a crisis demands the departure of a high official to some other part of the world, and the Secretary is pinned down in Washington, here is a colleague as prepared as he to respond. And so, in an infinite variety of situations including the physical disability of the Department's head, the Under Secretary stands shoulder to shoulder with the Secretary: an intimate sharer of his burdens *eo praesente*, his effective substitute *in absentia*. Entailed, thus, is a considerable overlapping of functions between the two, in which the *alter ego* becomes as preoccupied as the Secretary in all the latter's roles save management of the Department.

If there be a second Under Secretary, subordinate to the general Under Secretary, as from time to time there is, his position is created to deal with political or economic questions for which the two top officials consider themselves inadequately prepared or lacking sufficient time to handle. He is not available for internal management. All but one of the Deputy Under Secretaries are similarly occupied with substantive problems. The exception is the Department's principal administrative officer.

This is the Deputy Under Secretary for Administration. What of him? Is he not the official to whom management of the Department can be delegated? If administration means anything does it not mean management? And if the Department's chief administrator exists at so high a level, is he not, then, the manager?

It would seem so, but in fact this has not occurred. The

reasons are subtle. They have to do in part with the nature of diplomatic affairs, in part with the concept of administration held by the diplomatic establishment, in part with still other attitudes of the diplomatic mind, in part, finally, with Presidential unfamiliarity with the Department.

Diplomatic affairs involve the psychologies and interests of other peoples. Considerable knowledge of the politics, economies, cultures and even religions of other societies is demanded of any overall manager of the State Department. A profound familiarity with our own country, its philosophy, principles, character and resources is naturally also required, as well as a detailed knowledge of the techniques of diplomacy. Our diplomatic officers usually possess none of these things to the required extent. So no Secretary of State or President has been willing to trust one of them with the management of the Department. At the same time, while diplomatic officers have not themselves greatly aspired to such a role, neither have they been willing for an outsider to convert the post of Deputy Under Secretary for Administration into a position of general management.

The diplomatic officers hold administration in low esteem and look upon the administrative officers as "bureaucratic termites simply chewing their way into the diplomatic furniture," or as glorified janitors. This view of administration — in which one can detect the attitudes of the exclusive diplomatic fraternity — has produced two different, largely incompatible types of officers — diplomatic and administrative — selected by two different standards of education, experience and qualities of mind, operating in two different worlds, neither of which respects the other. The establishment is thus cursed with two different sets of rarely reconcilable outlooks. In such a situation, no administrative officer has been able to work himself into overall managerial responsibilities.

The dissatisfaction of Presidents with the Department's performance and their unfamiliarity with it have led to clumsy efforts to import the needed managerial competence from outside. After experimenting unsuccessfully with the resources of private industry, Presidents have experimented with a public administrator from the Civil Service Commission and an attorney of the Department of Justice. None of these individuals had had any previous experience with foreign affairs, none had been previously involved in diplomatic transactions, none had lived in foreign environments, and none had worked in the State Department itself. None brought the desired results. None lasted. Yet in each case precious time was invested and, in one, substantial funds, for the man attempted to prepare himself by extensive travel abroad.

If there is neither any other available official nor any combination of officials to whom the Secretary can delegate the managerial function, just who — or exactly what — does run the State Department?

CHAPTER 3

The Self-Winding Clock

REGARDLESS OF WHO is at its head, the State Department, like a self-winding clock, largely runs itself. It does this through the subtle operations of the diplomatic fraternity and by deeply ingrained procedures which produce, delay, or withhold decisions and actions no matter what political party is in power or what group of men are trying to direct it from the Federal summit.

Although seriously challenged since 1946 and now much weakened, the fraternity persists and its attitudes are widely shared throughout the diplomatic establishment. These in turn govern venerable operating procedures which regulate the Department's performance throughout all political vicissitudes. We have already touched upon the fraternity and its attitudes. We now must examine the procedures by which they operate.

The assigners of personnel, in determining who does what, obviously have great influence on State's performance. The Secretary himself can hope to have a voice in filling but a handful of positions close to him, and even in these he is restricted by Presidential appointments. The task of making other assignments is delegated to the Deputy Under Secretary for Administration, under whom there is an administrative staff to deal specifically with personnel matters.

This delegation of authority has been highly unsuccessful because it has always been sharply contested by the geographical and functional bureaus. Carrying as they do much of the burden of policy formulation and diplomatic action in Washington, these bureaus are confident that they know best the skills and experience their duties require. Moreover, as we have seen, the geographical bureaus, with their diplomatic officers, disdain and distrust the administrative process. Hence they not only exercise a veto over assignments by the administrative staff but actively seek out personnel themselves.

To this conflict of activity must be added an additional confusing factor, the aggressive search for "good" assignments by individual officers. Each officer has his eye on promotion and the Department has aggravated this preoccupation by its up-or-out decree. Even under the best circumstances, an officer would naturally want his next move to be the most advantageous one for his own career. But under pressure of the up-or-out policy he is excessively active, encouraging colleagues to snap up assignments intended for him, but which he does not want, edging out others pursuing the prize position he himself is after. And during each assignment he restlessly looks about, to see where he might go next.

Such a free-for-all is hardly calculated to produce a department capable of systematic results. The Department's needs, and especially its long-range ones, are often completely over-

looked by bureaus and officers concerned with their own particular interests. The consequence is not only that assignments are made which are detrimental to the Department's
overall needs; but also that the excessive energy of individual
and office ambitions disrupts operations, nourishes false standards of service, and exaggerates the covert particularism and
loyalties which the absence of an effective manager and a basic
plan permit in the first place.

Even the best efforts at effective organization are frustrated.
For instance, an office director could emerge so committed to
quality performance and so ingenious in Departmental manipulation as to be willing to challenge these chaotic assignment methods. He could gradually maneuver to his desk a
detail of officers possessing the specialized experience and
skills his area required. Left long enough in his position, he
might succeed in assembling an able team of men and women
only to find himself confronted by his Assistant Secretary
arguing as follows: "You have in your office a dispropor-
tionate array of talent. So we are better staffed to deal with
your part of our area than any other. This creates an unbal-
anced performance in my bureau. We must distribute this
talent more evenly. You give up So-and-So and So-and-So to
such-and-such." Instead of supporting office directors in a
zealous quest for talent and stimulating others to emulate
them, Assistant Secretaries thus penalized successful manipu-
lators, cutting them and their offices down to common size
and reducing the Department to a level of average performance. So it happened during a period of crisis in Cyprus, when
the Department needed all the brains and experience it could
get on that part of the world, its desk officer for the island was

a man who had had no previous exposure to Cypriot affairs and knew little or nothing about them. He had been dropped into the position for wholly extraneous reasons.

Why does an Assistant Secretary undercut his own operations in this manner? He does so in the interest of maintaining good relations with other Assistant Secretaries and the personnel hierarchy. For under the principle of rotation, every foreign service officer is up for assignment sooner or later, the career Assistant Secretary along with all the others. The person who genuinely seeks to man *all* his desks with the best available talent will acquire the reputation of running too zealous a raiding bureau and will soon find himself a target of retaliation. Almost invariably he will have a difficult time when his own assignment comes up. The Department's goal is not one of excellence but accommodation.

The rotation principle bears some responsibility for the baffling assignments frenzy. It decrees that an officer must change jobs as often as every two years and no less than every four or five. It is rare that he remains in the same place longer. Moreover, if he is a violinist, he must become a flute player; if a flutist, a drummer. This is what the Department calls developing "generalists," which is to say jacks-of-all-instruments and masters of none. The orchestra winds up with gifted violinists who can play the violin only moderately well because required to learn other instruments too. The quality of the orchestral performance inevitably suffers.

It is well to recall that the Department was not always so afflicted. Until 1954 it was primarily manned — like the other Executive departments — by a permanent corps of civil servants. These provided continuity and stability, a fixed group around which revolved the rotating diplomatic officers. Between Department and overseas posts a thin trickle of diplomats passed back and forth, stimulating the sedentary headquarters staff and carrying overseas a clearer awareness of headquarters' thinking and politics.

The arrangement had its defects. The control of the flow was largely in the hands of the inner fraternity of the diplomatic service and was used to favor the special "brothers." There was also friction between the stationary center and the rotating diplomatic officers, due less to the system than to the officers' attitudes. The defects could have been corrected by an adequate orientation and training of officers. In a word, difficulties could have been overcome if properly diagnosed and treated.

Diagnosed they were not but treated they assuredly were. In 1953 an Under Secretary — a political appointee — was horrified to discover that the diplomatic service, which had just been reduced in size by his Administration, on the ground that the establishment was overstaffed, was in fact too small. What could be a simpler and quicker technique of expansion than to merge civil servants with diplomats? This was decreed, and the decree summarily carried out.

A vast army of civil servants was suddenly uprooted from a settled life at home and packed off to a nomadic life abroad. Finding themselves far from home, trying to adapt to a life they neither knew nor desired, the carpet-baggers had to try to perform new functions, many of which they only dimly understood and were not trained to discharge. Most of them turned out to be square pegs in round holes. On the other hand, the cosmopolitan, polished diplomats abroad were brought back to what they considered routine, unadventurous chores in Washington.

Even in its more important positions the Department is now plagued by those disruptive rotations of personnel that were once limited to the overseas assignments. To be sure, a Secretary's intervention can occasionally keep a career officer at his post during a substantial part of the Secretary's own tour of duty. And a relatively few officers, such as Arabic area specialists and labor advisers, can contrive to serve for relatively long periods of time in geographical or functional assignments. But most officers are here this year, gone the next, carrying with them the experience gained in their positions, dissipating the hard-won insights and contacts which make policy-development and diplomacy work. The result is a disturbing vortex of change which endlessly sucks away continuity and drive.

With officers who are barely settled in one assignment beginning warily to explore future possibilities, the Department gets something less than profound concentration on the job at hand. This condition also places a premium on amicable relationships with other officers. In the constantly fluctuating personnel situation, one never knows when a colleague will be able to help or block a desired assignment. The psychological effects are obvious. It is safer to be wary than bold, more prudent to conform than to criticize. Officers tend to be compromisers rather than contesters, avoiders of argument rather than dynamic leaders. Since this cast of mind is carried over into representation of our national interests to foreign powers, it is clear that the Department is handicapped in two respects: first, in its own internal development of policy and diplomacy, and secondly, in its efforts to implement its decisions success-fully abroad.

One of the Department's most irritating characteristics — the peculiar degree to which its officers are reluctant to ac-knowledge inadequate performance — is partly attributable to this system of rotation. Officers are rarely in a job long enough to effect sizable changes. Denial of need for corrections is thus a temptation. Moreover, to admit the need of change would cast aspersions on predecessors — and who knows where predecessors will turn up some day? The chaos of rota-tion, in fact, assures a better-than-even chance that they will appear in some strategic position. Insistence upon change would also reflect on superiors. So, the prevailing characteris-tic of Departmental officers is to play it safe — deny anything is wrong or even improvable and move on to their next berths with a safe-conduct pass from satisfied superiors.

Even the abler officers who in a healthier environment would be inventive, knowing their tenure in a position to be limited, hesitate to introduce change they themselves cannot "wrap up." For a new idea, left for a successor to implement, may fail, and the originator himself be blamed. Rotation thus encourages concentration on minor adjustments and helps ex-plain why even the best of Department officers can be quick, perceptive and efficient in smaller, immediate things, but cau-tious, unoriginal, even indifferent and smugly conformist in larger, more far-reaching ones.

Another mystifying phenomenon is attributable to constant rotation. Most observers cannot understand why the Depart-ment sometimes sets out energetically on a good program, de-velops it for a while with excellent results and then lets it drift off inconclusively, eventually abandoning it entirely. This alternation of bursts of initiative and mystifying inactivity arises from the simple fact that an imaginative officer who had got himself in a position to command support for his ideas and been able to set them afloat has been transferred. It is not that he has committed any mistake or that his program has been proven unsound; his time has simply expired, rotation has swept him off and his successors have not been systematically selected for vision, skill, drive or equal familiarity with the problem.

Rotation explains another striking weakness — the tendency of the Department to repeat its mistakes endlessly. Whatever fresh insights frequent rotation may bring to individual officers and bureaus, it undermines the Department, by assuring that the bureaus most plagued by rotation can never permanently learn anything, can never accumulate an adequate reservoir of knowledge or intuition regarding any country, subject, or problem. What predecessors have once deduced from trial and error, successors must discover all over again. A rare exception may be found in the cases of diplomatic officers like Robert Murphy and Llewellyn Thompson, who were permitted to devote much of their careers to French or Soviet affairs respectively. In Thompson's case, wisdom was carried one step further. When he wanted to retire, he was persuaded to accept a position in the Department as "ambassador at large" to advise the Secretary and the President on Soviet problems.

A classic example of the effects of all this on a major program has been the Alliance for Progress. Similar programs were undertaken in Cuba and the Philippines after our war with Spain and subsequently in Latin America by a dynamic Coordinator of Inter-American Affairs, a political appointee by the name of Nelson Rockefeller. All their lessons were forgotten and their personnel dissipated. No comprehensive reports on the programs were ever requested of these men by the diplomatic establishment, nor did any "orientation" or training program analyze this earlier experience and transfer the results to successive waves of incoming officers. The later Alliance for Progress was initiated as though it came from the brow of Jove. It failed to take advantage even of the techniques, errors and successes of so recent an experiment as the Marshall Plan. So it is with each constructive projection of policy and diplomacy: it begins *de novo*, repeating earlier lapses and mistakes, and failing to acquire the appropriate focus and momentum from earlier experience.

Faltering is aggravated by another procedure, the "efficiency report," which is an annual evaluation of each officer's performance. This is a noble effort and, of course, is not uncommon. Every government employee is annually evaluated by his superior. But in the diplomatic establishment the procedure, like many another, operates in a peculiar environment and is permitted to exercise a far-reaching, disturbing, often devastating influence.

The ordinary civil servant's evaluation is brief and perfunctory; the diplomat's, lengthy and detailed. A diplomat's superior not only must answer a long list of queries about his subordinate's personality, character, intellect and competence, but also must add several pages of original characterization, so that promotion boards thousands of miles away in Washington, with little personal knowledge of officers, may judge who is deserving of advancement. Obviously, this is a difficult undertaking, highly vulnerable to subjective factors. Not only are each superior's own qualities involved, but also his degree of skill in putting his personal judgments into writing. Since judges must reach decisions solely on the basis of these literary portraits, the subjectivity of the judges themselves is likewise involved. Error and inequity inevitably occur.

The efficiency report procedure, we must remember, operates in a highly competitive situation. A civil servant can remain in his grade or position indefinitely. A diplomatic officer cannot. As we have noted, he goes up or out. In the weighing of efficiency reports, therefore, promotion boards must sometimes take account of very small differences in evaluations, even very small shadings of phrasing. This naturally means that efficiency reports must be works of art, in which very nice differences in language can have a potent effect. The desire to stand well with a supervisor, all too prevalent a factor in any human organization, thus becomes in the diplomatic establishment an exaggerated attribute contributing to cautious performance.

Consider now how further exaggeration of conformity and agreeableness is induced by the combined effects of rotation and efficiency reports. Serving with superiors for short — sometimes very short periods — officers are well aware of the impact on their careers of immediate impressions and many take refuge in the prompt cultivation of civilities whatever the cost in substantive performance or national interest. Short tenure of a position tempts every officer to show an extravagant affability in his short-lived relationships. Thus the efficiency report, combined with rotation, contributes to orienting the

establishment's performance toward a level of superficial ami-
ability.

Among the unfortunate consequences of all this has been
the reinforcement of the fraternity system, because of an elementary human reaction to excessive risk. The fraternity
serves as a protective device. In turn it uses the efficiency report as a protective device, so as to praise the "brothers" and
skillfully downgrade the "intruders." Since outside pressures
for better performance have forced into the establishment in-
fusions of non-fraternity talent at higher ranks, reactions of
the fraternity have split the establishment into fragments
which weaken that very morale and team action a Secretary —
and the nation — need. A few examples will demonstrate
how these phenomena reduce the effectiveness of even the
simplest processes of the Department.

Take the briefing of colleagues prior to their assumption of
new assignments. This is of primary importance, yet it is more
neglected than performed. Why? Knowledge is power. The
mistakes of one's competitors improve one's own chances of
advancement. So one is tempted to brief one's colleagues as
slightly as possible. This is a subtle means of reducing competition for promotion, and of course it is employed generally
against non-members of the fraternity. It obviously can have a
disastrous effect on the Department's performance.

The situation is similar for such an elementary technique for
coordination and stimulation as the staff meeting. An Assistant
Secretary, for instance, will indeed meet with his subordinates as often as three mornings a week. This sounds impressive as an operating device until one finds that too generally the Assistant Secretary tends only to pick his colleagues'

brains for information and opinions useful to *him* in his thrice-weekly meetings with the Secretary, neglecting to make himself useful to *them* — by informing them, stimulating them, pitching their thinking and action to higher, more dynamic levels.

Conversely, most participants in staff meetings are all too often reluctant to bring up matters of real importance. This was pointed out almost twenty years ago as characteristic of the Under Secretary's staff meetings. It is applicable to most meetings today, because few officers wish to appear less than omniscient or wish to invite poaching on their preserves.

Such factors add shading to the picture presented by phenomena noted earlier, such as the diplomatic officers' scorn of planning, research and intelligence. Functions like these are basic, intellectual functions. They insistently raise questions: How much do we know? Where can we find additional facts, points of view, interpretations, perspectives? What are the newest techniques of mobilizing, storing, classifying and retrieving information? How does one compare events between different nations or societies and through different time periods? How does one anticipate data not yet known and the probable courses of action of others? How does one order data with theoretical patterns that will help him understand whole classes of events? Such questions — and the functions they demand — can be dismissed or ignored only at great national risk. But such questions and functions — as well as the attitudes that make them possible — are foreign to officers who insist that they have all the answers.

As we have seen, an effort has been made to break down tidy geographic divisions by assigning officers to the geographic bureaus to perform functional roles. But if a politico-military, planning or economic officer is a diplomatic officer — and above all if he is a fraternity man — his impact can be weak. Through undue preoccupation with his promotion, he may placate the very bureau he is charged to stimulate, thereby failing to induce the broad-scaled, long-range thinking and intellectual give-and-take that is so badly needed to get our diplomatic effort off the ground.

Thus we can perceive a subtle weakness which runs through the whole establishment. Preparation and training of officers are directed by other officers. Assignment and promotion of officers are made by other officers. Efficiency reports — on which assignments, promotions and other personnel action rest — are written by colleagues. The inbreeding, nurtured by the fraternity (but not to be attributed exclusively to it), has been considerable; its effects have been far-reaching. Any deficiency in an officer's concept of foreign policy and diplomacy and the skills and attributes they require will inevitably be reflected in his evaluations of colleagues and of the needs of the establishment. Rating officers attaching antiquated importance to traditional skills — such as reporting, remaining on the sidelines, keeping one's nose clean — will extol the officers possessing them. Officers excessively cautious and discreet, excessively adept in avoiding "involvement" of their Government in an active, dynamic diplomacy, will be too often the ones to get ahead. They will even be assigned to critical areas, as the establishment's senior officers. On the other hand, officers with new skills and initiative, like those in labor and public affairs, who take risks and occasionally get their fingers burned, will be criticized and denied advancement or influence.

Notwithstanding such defects, the Department has never done very much to improve its ways. As for its method of evaluating officers it claims not to know how to improve it in any basic respects. Trapped by its defensive attitudes, it has tried to console itself with the idea that, for all its faults, the system is as good as human imperfection will permit. Nevertheless, the complaints of officers embittered by inequitable treatment have induced a certain amount of superficial experimentation. Congress itself has intervened from time to time to press for improvements. But adjustments have been of a tinkering nature and periodically reversed by rotation of officers.

One can now understand why the Secretary has such insuperable problems of management and delegation. Every operating procedure is intertwined with attitudes of mind, each inducing and reinforcing the other, all directed toward the negative goal of preserving "the system." Fresh ideas, fresh operating procedures which challenge the going ones in any basic sense, have too seldom been able to get off the ground. Tinkering, with constant clucking claims of "great improvements," goes on, and occasionally there is a little change here, a little change there, swinging in and out, periodically reversed. But a bedrock improvement fails to materialize because thorough analysis and planning are not encouraged in the operating bureaus, and when an officer comes along who is disposed to undertake it, he is not long enough in his position to accomplish anything of lasting value. Year in and year out, the Department has perpetuated its old ways, endeavoring to operate in a manner which not even time can honor.

CHAPTER 4

At Arm's Length

ONE OF THE MOST deeply rooted tenets of the State Department is that it alone should govern the formulation and, very largely, the execution of foreign policy. According to State, it alone has the experts. Instead of using and stimulating to the fullest the rest of the Federal establishment, therefore, State has tried to keep it at arm's length. Unfortunately, the "experts" of State are often far from expert. Furthermore, the plural interests and objectives of the Federal Government in its world relationships do not support the myth that the State Department can single-handedly or simply on its own initiatives bear the burden of conducting and coordinating our foreign affairs.

But State's attitude dies hard. Worldwide developments may have obliterated the demarcation between domestic and foreign affairs; the latter may penetrate every sector of government activity at home; and other components of the Federal Government may have become involved in foreign affairs as long ago as the 1930s. But no matter. It should not be that way. Close your eyes to it and maybe it won't be there. Or perhaps, better still, complain and grumble about it and perhaps somebody will do something to clear away the traffic, or at least give the highway controls to State. This, indeed, is what Presidents Eisenhower and Kennedy tried to do, although in diametrically opposite ways. President Johnson has reversed the Kennedy decision, but it remains to be seen whether he will go as far as Eisenhower in recognizing how heavy and complex the traffic is.

The rapid development of international organization, which occurred during the Second World War and which after the war swept us into an era of broad social commitment, should have created in the State Department, as it did in other components of the Federal establishment, a fresh definition of foreign affairs. For virtually the entire Federal apparatus of government was duplicated by an international apparatus. Paralleling national treasury departments and banking systems came an international complex of institutions and arrangements for financial management, including an international monetary fund and a world bank. Paralleling national agricultural departments came an international food and agricultural organization. National departments of health, education and welfare found international counterparts in a world health organization and a United Nations educational, scientific, and cultural organization. Aviation regulatory bodies have their counterpart in an international civil aviation organization, and atomic energy commissions in an international atomic energy agency. An older international labor organization, established in 1919 as a part of the League of Nations, continued to parallel labor departments, as did a universal postal union the national post-office departments.

These parallel national and international agencies, dealing

with the same kinds of problems, talking the same technical language, exchanging publications, trading ideas, sharing comparable experience, of course promptly engaged in much direct communication and negotiation. Only in this way could the international machinery in fact adequately serve the basic interests which had driven national governments to create it. But these direct relationships led to a diffusion of policies, initiatives and catalytic thinking across a wide arc of government. They made virtually every department and agency of Government a little State Department. The problem became not merely one of channeling all this broad-scaled collaboration through the State Department, but also one of acquainting diplomatic officers with all the varied and complex traffic, and of training them to draw upon it and guide it to full national advantage.

This problem State has done little or nothing about. In fact, it has never shown any awareness of the positive value in this pluralistic approach to world affairs. Instead of giving imaginative leadership in the Federal community, State has complained and grumbled, nursing a fearful, dog-in-the-manger attitude toward its sister agencies. It has resented the need for diversity and the sharing of power, dragging its feet on the training required and showing exasperation at the effort exacted to match minds with other departments which are often better informed and prepared to act in special fields than itself. It does not view the Federal community as a rich resource of specialized information and thought, research, policy initiative and diplomacy which, in the nation's interest, should be systematically nourished and tapped. Other departments and agencies are competitors, "rival claimants," somehow having "a different mission" from State's and intruding, unwanted, into foreign affairs. Indeed, one must wonder to what extent the State Department has regarded itself over the years as part of the Federal government.

State's aloofness bothered some of us a good deal in the hard years of McCarthyism, when the diplomatic establishment was being attacked for lack of security-consciousness. State left Senator McCarthy a number of openings. It indeed had been slack in security, so slack that during the Second World War the President used the military establishment for the communication of messages which normally would have gone — and should have gone — through diplomatic channels. The interest of a "brother" too often weighed more heavily in the minds of officers than the broad national interest. But McCarthy's attack was all the more devastating because of another factor: State simply could not elicit sympathy or support within the Federal community.

No one can deny that the operating procedures and the parochialisms of many components of the Federal Government present serious problems. Some of the commissions, moreover, lack positive direction, their chairmen being but presiding officers. When chairmanships revolve among several commissioners, the problem of direction is aggravated, because coupled with State's own vice of wholesale rotation. Agencies headed by a large number of commissioners contribute to further unwieldiness and inconclusiveness of policy. When subjected to heavy pressures from private interests, they advance compromises which meet neither our national nor our international needs. Some compound State's problems by failing to do forward planning. In other words, the State Department is not alone in possessing deficiencies. Its difficulties are found elsewhere, too, and they accentuate State's own weaknesses.

Furthermore, the fact that the Executive branch of the government has proliferated in pragmatic fashion, without plan or design, has complicated the problem. It has come to resemble the collection of barns, shacks, silos, tool sheds and garages of an old farm. As a result, along with regular Cabinet departments, there cluster around the President numerous boards, commissions, administrations, authorities and corporations. This would be onerous enough for a department of foreign affairs, but in addition there are agencies independent of the President which do not cluster around him at all, constituting what has been called "a new and headless 'fourth branch' of the Government."

That this situation sharply challenges any department trying to coordinate our approach to foreign affairs, goes without saying. Such coordination may be impossible. The nearest approximation to a solution may rest not in a department but in the office of the President. State insists, however, that the coordinating role in foreign affairs belongs to it.

What is the basis of this insistence?

There is none in the Constitution. The only reference in that document to Executive management of foreign affairs is in connection with the President. He is put in charge.

Legislation has not modified this Constitutional directive. The original Act of Congress setting up the State Department recognized the President as supreme in the coordinating role, and the basic authority of the Department has not changed since that Act. Even when granting substantive power to the Secretary of State from time to time, Congress has explicitly stipulated that he "shall act under the direction of the President." Hence, the Chief Executive has not only the supreme power over our foreign relations, but also the right to determine what kinds and degrees of delegation he will make and to what departments.

Chief executives have varied considerably in this delegation. In regard to State, they have shifted from one end of the spectrum to the other. Some have been known to appoint a Secretary of State on the express understanding that he keep out of foreign affairs altogether, leaving them entirely to the President.

Nonetheless, State's claim to a coordinating role seems logical on the surface. Must not a busy President turn to some department or agency to discharge this duty? If so, to which would he more logically turn than to the department originally set up to assist him in the conduct of the nation's foreign relations?

The answer to this, of course, is that political power does not accrue to any group of men according to logic, but only according to that group's capacity to assume responsibility.

Why has State failed to understand this simple fact?

The reasons are partly historical. At the beginning of our government four departments were established — Foreign Affairs, War, Treasury and Justice. As first to be established, Foreign Affairs, or State as it came shortly to be called, was regarded as the ranking Department. For this relatively insignificant reason its Secretary was eventually prescribed by law to follow the Vice President in line of Presidential succession. This primacy in the Cabinet was embroidered by the prestige and protocol of the international society in which top officials of our government mingled — a social factor, no more, but of potent psychological and political impact. By this extra-constitutional evolution the Secretary of State came to be regarded as prime among Cabinet equals.

Since external affairs were for many years of little interest to other civilian departments, State came to exercise a virtual monopoly in dealings with foreign powers. The philosophy of civilian preeminence combined with the primacy of the Secretary of State in the Cabinet to give State supremacy over the military in foreign affairs. One can thus trace through historical and philosophical factors the subtle transition from the personal primacy of the Secretary of State to that of his department in the conduct of foreign relations.

This in turn led the State Department to assume an attitude of general superiority in the Federal establishment — an attitude fortified by other factors which we have already examined. State came to assume, as an operating hypothesis, that regardless of its ability to understand the national and international problems which constituted "foreign affairs," and to coordinate a complex Federal involvement in those affairs, it somehow had a Providential dispensation to control that involvement. Other hypotheses reinforced this one: that no other department or agency had much of a real interest in foreign affairs, and if it did have it shouldn't; that if a valid interest were asserted, the thing to do was not to understand it and coordinate it but circumscribe and even circumvent it; that the rest of the Federal Government was simply a nuisance to earnest, dedicated, all-knowing diplomatic officers. Consequently confusion has arisen in the Federal establishment during the last quarter-century as to where the coordinating function in our foreign relations should be placed if it is to be discharged effectively.

Coordination means harmonizing action. But decisions are required as to what action should be undertaken. These also must be harmonized or, better still, integrated. Prior to World War II (or perhaps one should say prior to the New Deal, before a worldwide depression obliterated so many distinctions between national and foreign affairs) integration of advice on foreign policy from all parts of the Executive branch was no problem. It was effected by the President or the Secretary of State in a personal, informal way. In both integration of advice and coordination of action, a word from the Secretary of State, as has been said, "carried with it a quality of Olympian majesty which usually evoked a quick response."

As World War II approached, however, foreign affairs had a sharper and sharper impact upon the nation; they became increasingly complex; State failed to keep abreast; and Federal agencies multiplied. Among the latter were some that thrust into foreign affairs, some in fact being set up explicitly to enter into discussions with foreign governments, to negotiate and make agreements with them, to iron out differences in interpretation of agreements, reach compromises when necessary — in a word, to make foreign policy and carry it out. All these functions constituted "dabbling" and "interfering" from the State Department's point of view, and great confusion from anybody's point of view, but they were activities the Department was rightly considered unequipped to perform. With State manifesting little or no desire to assume these extensive emergency tasks and showing little interest in preparing its officers to do so, the President of necessity looked elsewhere.

Hence, from the late 1930s on, the Department's position

in foreign affairs drifted further and further from center. When war struck, that position rapidly worsened. Major political and military relationships with our principal allies were handled directly by the President, with extensive use of personal representatives. The allied military commands worked closely together. So did the wartime civilian agencies with their opposite numbers. An Economic Defense Board and its successors operated at home and abroad, as did an Office of War Information. An Office of Strategic Services negotiated with foreign governments and underground movements, gathered intelligence and struck at the enemy. A dynamic Office of Coordinator of Inter-American Affairs, although placed in the State Department, was a free-swinging, virtually autonomous office. The Secretary of State was often not even invited to participate in international conferences convoked by the President for negotiation of important political issues; instead he was obliged abjectly to inquire around Washington later to find out what had gone on.

While State increasingly complained about all this, it believed that the problem was caused by depredations of the President and other agencies rather than new demands of the times and its own inadequacies. The Department as a whole responded to the competitive sensibilities and snobbishness of its individual officers, and it failed to press for adequate supplementation of its resources and effective training. Hence when belatedly it put up a fight for its claimed role of prime coordinator of foreign affairs, it found itself producing only an operational squabble. Self-defensively, the Secretary of State took to eulogizing his establishment, which only made matters worse, for the eulogy encouraged the nursing of grievances rather than the analysis of causes. Observing this, the Presi-

dent appointed not State but the Director of War Mobilization as coordinator and settler of conflicts in foreign economic
affairs. The coordination of foreign political and military
affairs remained the province of the President and his staff.

Thus ended State's bid for a central role in the administration and coordination of foreign affairs in wartime. Unable to
exert much influence in all these areas, the Department
turned considerable attention to the important but less immediate problem of postwar planning. This planning, as it developed, concerned only the international community, principally the form of organization which a United Nations should
assume. The Department neglected the larger problem of improving itself and its management of foreign affairs. It comforted itself with the thought that, once the war was over,
things would go back to where they had been some years before: a small, elite diplomatic community would resume its
sway, and the nod of its Secretary would regain its Olympian
majesty.

But things never did go back to where they once had been.
After the war, when State started once more arguing its traditional thesis, it carried little weight. In 1946, one of its officials expressed the essence of State's postwar thinking before a
Congressional committee in these terms:

> The Department of State, under the direction of the Presi-
> dent, in cooperation with Congress is responsible for the
> achievement of our foreign policy objectives. Other Govern-
> ment agencies, such as War, Navy, Treasury, Commerce and
> Agriculture departments, are also concerned with foreign rela-
> lations. . . . Effective coordination under the Department
> of State of all foreign relations activities is essential if we are
> to achieve our foreign policy objectives.

One detects in this simple, cure-all line of thought a cause of many of State's postwar difficulties both within its own diplomatic community and with other departments and agencies, the President and Congress.

Was the State Department in fact "responsible for the achievement of our foreign policy objectives?" By virtue of what? What legislation? What Presidential order? Were not other departments also responsible? If financial objectives were involved was not the Treasury Department generally responsible for their achievement? Had not the entire Federal community recognized this by according to Treasury the chairmanship of the Inter-Agency Advisory Council on International Financial Problems? If the objectives were agricultural, was not their achievement generally assigned to the Agriculture Department; if labor, to the Labor Department; if commercial, to the Commerce Department; and so on?

Furthermore, were "other Government agencies," such as those mentioned by the spokesman of State, simply "concerned" with foreign relations? Were they not, in fact, conducting a substantial part of these affairs? Were they not active parts of the entire Federal operation? And was not their activity in foreign relations, including negotiations, as valuable as State's?

Not only was the spokesman's contention that "effective coordination under the Department of State of all foreign relations activities is essential if we are to achieve our foreign policy objectives" based on dubious historical authority, but the earliest postwar experience also convinced other departments that State was simply not up to the coordinating role. They could see more and more examples of the Department's inability to grasp the whole of the government's problems and to mobilize its entire resources.

In training, for instance, State's deficiencies were obvious. Continuing to beg the question of what is meant by "effective coordination," State failed to prepare its officers to provide just that.

Secretaries of State began to reach outside for businessmen to jack up the Department's performance. Congress pressed for an augmentation of its skills and resources. While State's representative was trying to peddle his clichés on Capitol Hill, the President himself entered the picture.

As Senator, Mr. Truman had become aware of the need for better coordination of the government's sources of information and the fact that the need had become acute in foreign affairs. He had come to feel that "if there had been something like coordination of information in the government it would have been difficult, if not impossible, for the Japanese to succeed in the sneak attack at Pearl Harbor." As President, he found himself similarly situated. "Reports came across my desk on the same subject at different times from the various departments, and these reports often conflicted." He moved to improve things by proposing a centralized intelligence organization.

When he turned to State for advice, that Department took the position that centralization of information on foreign affairs rightfully belonged to it. Logically, this was so. And, logically, the President gave it this role. But it fumbled so badly he reversed himself and set up an interdepartmental intelligence authority responsible to him. This was the most "practical way," he felt, "for keeping the President informed as to what was known and what was going on." State was a part of the authority but it was denied a coordinating role.

The President felt the need also of "one top-level permanent setup in the government to concern itself with advising the President on high policy decisions concerning the security of the nation." This time he created a separate agency, under his own chairmanship — the National Security Council. Once more State should have read the signals.

As we have noted, two objectives must be achieved by any successful national effort in foreign affairs. One is the integration of consistent but flexible policies. This includes the development of a basic plan and the maintenance of its currency in changing international situations. The other objective is the mobilization of all the contributions needed to bring those policies into play in as many ways as possible, in every country of the world. To achieve these ends, a government must use all its resources of research, analysis and imagination, all its differing perspectives and specialized insights, all its operational techniques and its contacts with governments and peoples around the globe.

While writers in the field of foreign policy speak much of such integration and coordination, they say little about other, equally important functions which must be performed if integration and coordination themselves are to be achieved. The simplest and most elementary is exposing bureaucratic minds throughout the government to available information and ideas in the foreign affairs area. To perform this function regular, systematic consultation among them is required. Such a technique must also allow the interests and concerns of all parts of the government to be expressed, and policies and moves to be freely suggested, so that all parts of the Federal community can contribute, not only when the pressures of a crisis are greatest but at regular intervals, as a normal process of government. Only in this way can the various parts of a sprawling, complicated bureaucracy evolve an overall view, achieve operational insight and acquire a sense of timing — all of which would give rise to a true consensus, which would in turn be the basis of true "integration" and "coordination."

The significance of this is profound. For it is not through a power to command that any one department of the Government can play the roles of integrator and coordinator. Regardless of any "primacy" in foreign affairs that State may have acquired over the years, other departments will not permit historical precedent to give State sole command on matters so vital to them and to national survival. Even if State had done more — or if it should try to do more in the future — to prepare itself to play these roles, it could do so only by a systematic approach, productive of a Federal consensus.

Closely associated with the function of systematic consultation is the need for leadership to stimulate ideas and action — what one might call the mobilizing function. Active encouragement of diversity of thought and approach in foreign affairs has become crucial to our survival. The rich resources of our pluralistic society must somehow be brought to bear upon an equally pluralistic world society. Only by keeping our entire governmental apparatus sensitive and active can this be done, and our free society meet the challenge of managed societies, particularly those with great populations and immense economic, nuclear and political power. While Secretaries of State face in their own department the problem of overcoming rigid hierarchies so that ideas and action can rise from below, the government faces the comparable problem of stimulating exchange of ideas among coequal departments. If State wishes to play the role of integrator-coordinator, it must take the lead in solving this problem.

How has the State Department offered to do so? Only through the casual contacts of its officers with their opposite numbers in other departments, the assignment of a handful of diplomatic officers to a few other agencies, an insignificant effort by the Foreign Service Institute to give a few officers a superficial knowledge of the Federal establishment, and a poorly organized system of inter-agency committees and organizational gadgets.

For most of its contacts with the rest of the Executive branch, State has traditionally relied upon the officers of its pyramidal mass. Through their individual contacts occurs much of the consultation and concurrence required in State's transactions. Although daily and numerous in the aggregate, these contacts are rarely sustained on any one subject or in any one area. They have never been organized to produce any systematic approaches to problems or anticipatory analyses. Being no more than off-the-cuff conferences, they are inadequate for achieving integration, coordination, mobilization and consensus.

It was only after World War II that State, stimulated by Congress, began to experiment with the assignment of diplomatic officers to other departments. Congress's thought was that this would broaden State's horizons, and those of other departments as well. It was a sensible idea, but State has used the statutory authority Congress provided to engage in this experiment with customary conservatism. Its officers have felt strongly that such assignments would remove them from the mainstream of promotion, so they have resisted them. When competitiveness was intensified by introduction of the "up or out" rule and the fraternity took care to spare its favorite brothers such assignments, resistance mounted especially high. Officers perceived that they ran not only the risk of "out of sight, out of mind" but suffered the visible brand of not "belonging." If unsuccessful in maneuvers to avoid such assignments, officers began immediately to lay plans for an early return to the Department or to a detail overseas. This was hardly calculated to develop the technique into useful dimensions. By no orientation or training has State changed, or even endeavored to change, this attitude.

For a more sustained approach to the rest of the Federal Government, State has relied upon the device of inter-agency committees. These consist of representatives of various agencies possessing an interest in a given subject or area. Some committees have been created by Congress, others by the President; in both cases they are generally presided over by members of departments other than State and are not subject to the State Department's control. These types of committees are regarded favorably by other agencies, but they present problems to State in its efforts to play the role of coordinator.

The great bulk of the inter-agency committees are improvised by State. Membership is rarely offered to all those agencies truly involved but rather to those which State deems itself justified in inviting, and the justification is all too often in terms of the late 1920s or early 1930s. Moreover, there is a general attitude in State that other agencies and departments are competitors rather than collaborators, possessing a "mere curiosity" rather than a real stake in foreign affairs, and that they desire committee membership as a "form of status seeking." In State's view, inter-agency committees are "a principal cause for the delays and difficulties in the operation of policy-making machinery"; hence, when the Department is left to make its own decision, the technique is used in the most sporadic way possible.

This attitude is, of course, stultifying. Committees tend to come into existence only when a crisis or serious problem has already emerged, and subside as the more urgent elements of the crisis momentarily fade.

Here and there, coordination has been sought by the creation of a new position designed to bring into focus some agency's liaison with the Department. In recent years, a Coordinator of International Labor Affairs has been attached to the summit. The position of Deputy Assistant Secretary for Politico-Military Affairs has been created. But these are operating devices that do little more than facilitate the transaction of day-to-day business. Even when supplemented by an Inter-Departmental Planning Group and a Research Coordination Group — both belatedly set up in 1964 — they do not perform the broad clearing-house and consensus-building functions so desperately needed in the Federal bureaucracy. Nor do they provide the overall positive leadership which is the basis of effective integration of policy and coordination of operations.

The inadequacy of these various approaches by State has forced three Presidents to take the lead in strong remedial measures. President Truman, as we have noted, led off with the creation of an inter-agency committee known as the National Security Council. Six years later President Eisenhower added the Operations Coordinating Board. As promptly as Eisenhower had established the OCB, President Kennedy abolished it. Just a year ago, President Johnson created the Senior Interdepartmental Group to try to fill the vacuum.

The National Security Council, which consists of but a few members of the Cabinet, meets under the chairmanship of the President, not the Secretary of State. It meets at the initiative of the President, and he sets its agenda. It provides him with a source of prompt, collective advice and information on the more critical issues and problems affecting national security.

This has been the Council's positive contribution. Its limitations have been equally great. It deliberates under pressure, discussing crucial problems hastily, as they arise. It deals with crises rather than their causes and thus does little to anticipate problems or to nip them in the bud. It elaborates no basic plan or strategy. Furthermore, it neither decides anything, this being the President's prerogative, nor implements the President's decisions, this remaining the responsibility of the respective executive departments and agencies.

The gravity and complexity of questions presented to the Council, the immediacy with which they must be considered and the heavy pressures upon its members limit both the accuracy of their advice and the effectiveness of their departments' follow-up. Cordell Hull observed long ago that the "tremendous increase in the duties and problems of the . . . Government made it difficult, if not well-nigh impossible, for each Cabinet member to keep up with all the important questions arising in the entire field of Government so as to render

prompt opinions, outside the affairs of his own department."
It was no easier in 1947. It has been no easier since.

Council members should be able to weigh our resources and
the repercussions of policies and actions outside their own departments. The interests of Labor, Commerce, Agriculture
and others should be taken into consideration; and the resources and contributions of each must be calculated. But no
Cabinet members save the Secretaries of State, Defense and
Treasury are Council members and attend regularly. This
quintessence of the Cabinet therefore has, in advising the
President, the formidable responsibility of conjecturing the
total interests and resources of the Federal Government. But
who in the Council is competent to give advice about, say, the
capacity of labor organizations at home and abroad to help
achieve our foreign policy objectives? Who can give advice on
student organizations? Who, on other occupational and mass
organizations? Yet such organizations are involved in crises,
for they are all sources of social unrest and leadership, as well
as communist targets, in areas vital to our national security.
An adequate State Department might have enabled the Secretary of State to help fill such vacuums, but not a Department that sees Federal agencies as "rival," "competing,"
"fouling."

It was in these respects that serious weaknesses of the
Council appeared. It failed to tap Federal resources fully. It
did not anticipate crises and problems. It failed to mobilize —
indeed it did not know — all the subtle influences which the
total Federal establishment could provide, for keeping some
problems from becoming crises, and for doctoring others out
of existence. In addition, inadequate follow-up made initial

decisions ineffectual. Council members, as hard-pressed officials, had perforce to delegate the execution of Presidential
decisions, and departments and agencies not represented on
the Council got their information and directives secondhand,
if at all.

As the military mind of Marshall had seen the need of creating an apparatus for assuring more prompt and systematic
follow-through of his decisions within his own department, so
President Eisenhower's sought similar assurance for his decisions in the total Federal establishment. Accordingly, in 1953,
under the National Security Council he established the Operations Coordinating Board. This was an instrumentality to assure that all dimensions of a problem expected to come before
the Council were examined in advance. It was also intended
to provide methodical carrying out of a Presidential decision,
with systematic consideration of its application beyond the
immediate crisis or country to which it related.

The board was presided over by the Under Secretary of
State, thus formally recognizing, for the first time in recent
history, the central position claimed by the State Department
in the development and execution of foreign policy. While in
the National Security Council the Secretary of State was but
one of several members, in the Operations Coordinating
Board, his deputy was in the driver's seat. Fellow passengers
were the Deputy Secretary of Defense, the Directors of the
Central Intelligence Agency, the United States Information
Agency and the economic and technical assistance agency
(called in those days the International Cooperation Administration), and the President's own special assistant for national
security affairs.

The membership of the OCB was therefore broader than that of the NSC, and even more departments were involved in the germination of ideas and policies at lower levels. Functioning through country committees on which were represented most of the departments and agencies involved in foreign affairs, the OCB assured that each general policy directive of the President was applied to every country of the world and that this implementation had the benefit of suggestions of policy and diplomacy from the greater part of the Federal Government. Over each of these country committees presided a representative of State, again acknowledging the diplomat's claim to central responsibility in foreign affairs.

Being under a Presidential agency — the Security Council — rather than under a department, the OCB was in a unique position to act as a clearinghouse and to mobilize resources. In many instances, its country committees did this admirably. Their systematic, country-by-country, subject-by-subject review of policy for the first time made available to those who were developing American foreign policy and diplomacy, the vast resources of the Federal community. Ideas generated ideas, suggestions bred suggestions. No open and constructive mind participating in these committees could have failed to be stirred and enriched.

For the first time in our history, the Federal Government came reasonably close to reconciling the needs for diversity and unity in the development of our foreign policy and diplomacy. For the first time, a nearly complete mobilization of Federal resources was brought to bear upon that policy and its execution. A way had been finally devised of assuring a careful enough study of every country of the world to uncover problems and needs before they became crises and to evolve basic, long-range policies. The Federal establishment began to look and plan ahead in unison.

In addition, the OCB-NSC system helped State remedy a number of its own internal deficiencies. By generating country-by-country memoranda, OCB improved State's slipshod briefing of officers prior to their overseas assignments. Officers finally knew what the United States was trying to accomplish, systematically, in each country. As early drafts of memoranda were sent to our missions abroad for comment — and final drafts eventually sent as instructions — they brought the far-flung field posts in closer touch not only with the thinking of the Department, but also with that of the President and of the whole Federal government. Being developed by all interested departments and agencies and known to them, these memoranda more effectively bound their representatives abroad, thereby providing a tool for easing the ambassadors' burden of coordination within their missions.

Moreover, State's policy planning staff was tied in directly to the NSC-OCB staff. Thus, a technique had been devised of placing State's planning office in a central position, capable of exercising a truly radial influence throughout the Department and the whole Federal establishment. This in itself was a master stroke.

Most important of all, however, the accumulation of NSC-OCB studies and policy-diplomacy recommendations soon constituted the basic foreign policy program which State itself had failed to produce and which the entire Federal community urgently needed. Being produced by a government-wide process, rather than by a single department, programs contained few departmental parochialisms. Its elements were suitable for use by the whole Federal establishment. Furthermore, participation in the creation of the program gave each agency an understanding of the interests, resources and roles of the others.

All State had to do was to exercise the leadership handed to it by the President. It now could play the very role it had long and bitterly complained at being denied. But it was precisely in State that the system wavered and eventually fell.

The Department saw the OCB as it tends to see all innovation — less as an opportunity than as a disturbing departure from routine. Moreover, the OCB committees contested the Department's exclusive attitude, confronted it more sharply than ever before with "rival claimants" and obliged it to consort more intimately with the Federal "hacks" it had always tried to keep at arm's length. So it saw the OCB committees not as a providential means of developing a Federal consensus and a basic foreign policy and diplomacy, but simply the addition of more meetings to calendars, more hours to be consumed in trading ideas, more time to be spent reducing ideas to written recommendations and instructions. It never saw in these things the techniques of leadership.

This attitude all too soon was reflected in State's representation on the committees. Originally, the thought was to have the highest possible committee leadership, which meant office directors of State. A few people in State appreciated this and implemented it. When they did, committees were generally well run, providing the desired results. But many offices fell to sending subordinates, even the lowest-ranking one — the country desk officer. Chiefs thus gave way to Indians and Indians failed to lead. There were even some Indians who took a sardonic attitude toward the exercise, deriding and stifling instead of encouraging it.

All in all, State's reaction to the Eisenhower process made it evident that the Department was simply not constituted or prepared — in attitudes, skills, operating procedures — to play effectively the role it claimed in the Federal establishment. Its negative reactions reached influential ears in a way that condemned not itself but the system of coordination the President had handed to it. One of the first decisions of President Kennedy, accordingly, was to strike down the OCB.

The needs which the OCB filled remained. While State was inclined to fall back upon its individual officers and unsystematic inter-agency committees, it was forced by crises and Presidential pressures to experiment with the technique of the emergency "task force," which is simply an inter-agency committee under another name, whose vitality rises and falls with the degree of immediate peril. When the more hazardous aspects of a crisis subside, the task force disbands, leaving nothing of interdepartmental character to deal systematically with the remaining problems.

As this became apparent, the uneasiness of Kennedy's successor grew. Preoccupied though he was with domestic and international crises, President Johnson saw the need of reverting to something like the OCB process. For analysis and advice he turned, significantly, not to State, but to a general in the Army, as Truman had done. This time, however, the general was not Secretary of State but simply a student of the problem and proposer of a solution.

On March 4 a year ago, the President announced his adoption of General Maxwell Taylor's proposals. A permanent interdepartmental committee was established, called the Senior Interdepartmental Group and headed by the Under Secretary of State as an "executive chairman." Under SIG were established other committees known as Interdepartmental Regional Groups (IRG), headed by geographic Assistant Secretaries of State.

The SIG, said the President's announcement, is to "function as a focal point for decisions and actions on overseas interdepartmental matters which are referred to it by the Secretary of State or by an Assistant Secretary of State, or raised by the action of an individual member." The "executive chairman" designation is intended to confer upon the Under Secretary the authority to "decide all matters" coming before the Senior Group, subject to the right of any member to appeal from his decision to higher authority. The President's statement emphasized that "this is an important provision which makes the difference between the normal committee and an incisive, decision-making body."

Other regular members of SIG are the Deputy Secretary of Defense, the heads of AID, USIA and CIA, the Chairman of the Joint Chiefs of Staff and the Special Assistant to the President for National Security Affairs. Representatives of other departments and agencies are to attend meetings when deemed to have an interest in matters under consideration and are to "have the same right as the regular members when their business is being considered." Any department or agency not a member may raise matters for action by SIG.

What the relationship of the new Groups will be to the National Security Council and to the Department's planning staff was not announced. It is therefore not clear what the new committees will contribute to the integration of foreign policy. Nor is it clear whether the new system will contribute as effectively as the OCB to the exposure of the Federal bureaucracy to all available information and thinking on foreign affairs, to systematic consultation and stimulation and to the development of a Federal consensus. The likelihood is that it cannot because of restricted participation. Whether it will evolve a basic program we must wait to see. Thus, its ability to contribute to the solution of the perennial and pressing problem of coordination will be uncertain for some time. The attitudes and procedures of the State Department will have much to do with these questions and if the Department fails again to measure up it will assuredly invite further criticism and moves by the President.

One thing is clear: Presidential orders are not enough. The Chief Executive can issue any decrees he wants, but the pressures of international problems, the demands from all over the world upon all segments of the Federal Government and the sustained relationships which all those segments have with Congress and international affairs will defeat every effort toward integration and coordination which does not have the support of a systematic, government-wide consensus-building process guided effectively by the State Department or by some other agency.

CHAPTER 5

The Word and
the Sword

DIPLOMACY TODAY REFLECTS — and will long reflect — the
environment of force brought into the world by fascist and
communist dictators. This is not to say that force was absent
from international relations before, but only that today it is
deliberately, ideologically directed to the destruction of democratic society and the order and freedom that make democracy
possible. We thus stand in the position of ancient Athens.
Communist and fascist strategy, like that of Philip of Mace-
don and Alexander the Great, being based upon all available
means of extinguishing freedom of choice — even in purely
cultural matters — imposes upon free nations the burden of
mobilizing all their own resources for defense. A crucial weakness of the State Department has been its unwillingness and
inability to effect this mobilization.

This weakness in the military area has remained obscured
from the general public, and from most members of the diplomatic establishment as well. The relations of the State Department with the military have all too often appeared far better than they have been in fact. One reason for this is that

external danger has borne heavily upon State-military relations, obliging the two establishments to gloss over many of
their differences and work together. Quite apart from any intrinsic ability of State to lead, the cold war and war itself — as
in Korea and Vietnam — have forced a merger of at least
some of the more urgent diplomatic and military elements of
defense.

But danger can also make concealed differences erupt into
sharp disputes. Why has it not done so in this particular set of
relationships? Historical and philosophical factors provide a
partial explanation. One such factor is the principle of civilian
control of the military. While the military — openly on some
occasions and covertly on others — has been known to take the
lead in foreign affairs, the principle of civilian supremacy has
always been present as a check upon this initiative. It has provided the rationale whereby State, not the military, has ulti-
mately had the final word. Whereas among civilian agencies
considerable question may exist concerning State's role in foreign affairs, none exists, in principle at least, for the military.

A second factor is the similarity of the history of State and
the military. The diplomatic and military establishments
came into existence with the Federal Government itself.
They are thus original, "old line" establishments. They represent no new approaches or philosophies of government.
They have required of one another no major adjustments in
attitudes, as have the Labor Department, or Health, Education and Welfare, or the Information and Central Intelligence
Agencies. Neither has riled the other to the same degree as
other components of the government by apparent "status
seeking," "itch to get into the act," or competition for power
without acknowledged responsibility. This has not prevented

some old-time diplomats, however, from being riled and feeling that the "military, after paddling in the pond of diplomacy for nearly a quarter of a century, should be invited to go dry their feet."

Military "paddling in the pond of diplomacy" began, in fact, with the beginning of the nation itself. Prowling the seven seas from our earliest years, naval officers were often obliged to bargain with foreign authorities. Bargaining was sometimes local and *ad hoc*, sometimes formal, rising to the level of treaties, as in the well-known case of Commodore Perry, who not only parleyed the reopening of Japan to foreign intercourse but negotiated the formal agreement giving legal effect to his *de facto* accomplishment. The same is true of the army, and to a lesser extent the marine corps. The air force in recent years has been almost as active as the navy since it has not only had bases to gain abroad but effective, day-to-day operations to negotiate with overseas labor unions and national authorities.

This involvement led to training for a broad range of international responsibilities and training led, in turn, to greater responsibilities. Our war with Spain provided a notable stimulus in this direction, leading Secretary of War Elihu Root over sixty years ago to spearhead a reorganization of the army to prepare officers more adequately for political duties. This initiated a powerful influence toward the training of army officers for greater involvement in foreign affairs, which, though subtle for many years, led to better formal training in international affairs than the diplomats themselves received. This was the point at which the diplomats began to fall noticeably behind.

The writings and teachings of a thoughtful naval officer, Alfred Mahan, contributed to this development. They stimulated the navy and gradually the military establishment as a whole to conceptualize a worldwide strategy combining diplomatic with military action. The State Department was totally outside this strong intellectual current of *realpolitik*. It had no Alfred Mahan, and even had it generated one, it possessed no training academy to provide him with a teaching podium. In the midst of these invigorating developments within the military establishment, State ambled along, scorning any professionalization of diplomacy, letting its officers assume their assignments with but a smattering of training, often unbriefed and forced to improvise.

When thrown up against the military, therefore, the diplomatic officers could hardly play a leading role. As one of them, Willard Beaulac, has written, when assigned as chargé d'affaires to Haiti in 1927 to serve under an American general who was the high commissioner there, he went inadequately briefed by State and was compelled to feel his way cautiously; he therefore decided he must conform to "the sort of thing that my predecessor had been doing." The trouble was, as he discovered when examining his predecessor's files for guidance, that that worthy "had been doing very little," he, too, having been trapped in a like quandary. So the chargé did little, concluding, in his unprepared condition, that the best he could do was "to look wise, try to understand what was going on, nod sagely at appropriate times, and, very occasionally, make a suggestion when matters involving State Department policies, concerning which I knew next to nothing, arose." State has performed in this manner all too often, and consequently all too frequently has played second fiddle to the better trained, better prepared, more resourceful military.

After being drawn into the diplomatic pond of the Paris

Peace Conference in 1919, our military officers participated in the occupation of Germany, adding the Rhineland to a list of overseas occupational experiences which already included Peking, Cuba, Puerto Rico, the Philippines, Murmansk and Panama. Thereafter, they took part in disarmament conferences of the 1920s and early 1930s, as they had earlier in the Hague Conferences of 1899 and 1907. They were given the responsibility of restoring order and devising ways of holding a free election in Nicaragua in 1929.

One might take any number of individual officers to illustrate the extent of this involvement. Frank R. McCoy is as good an example as any. A graduate of West Point, McCoy was called upon to superintend the Nicaraguan intervention under the guidance of the Secretary of State, to direct the Red Cross relief in Japan after the 1933 earthquake, to serve on the commission to conciliate the Chaco dispute between Bolivia and Paraguay and, as a member of the Lytton Commission of the League of Nations, to investigate Japanese belligerency in Manchuria. This constituted a good deal of "paddling in the pond of diplomacy" and one might suggest that all the tasks entrusted to McCoy might well have been delegated to diplomatic officers had they been similarly well trained.

The Japanese aggressions in the Far East and the rise of Hitler in Europe caused the military to intensify its planning for contingencies, including war itself. This rarely brought the military establishment into association with State, which had no planning staff, and no inclination to plan. When an exceptional danger arose, such as the possibility of Nazi infiltration into the American continent, an *ad hoc* State-military relationship developed. From such a relationship might evolve a liaison committee, consisting of the Under Secretary of State, the Chief of Naval Operations and the Army Chief of Staff, but this was uncommon. Furthermore, because such a committee represented no systematic interest it fell apart as the danger passed, leaving the underlying problems of State's relations with the military but superficially touched.

At the beginning of the war in Europe, State facilitated military operations in a number of ways. *Sub rosa* discussions between our military and the British eventually charged it with the task of putting the final civilian touches on the swap of destroyers for military bases and subsequently steering the agreement through Congress. The Secretary of State had the leading role in negotiations with the Japanese and played it with skill. While the public never understood the purpose of such protracted pourparlers, ignorantly criticizing Hull and the Department for prolonging them when they seemed useless, State was responding to a military desire to avoid a showdown with Japan for which we were not prepared and which could only detract from our support of Britain against Germany. Again, for strategic military reasons State bore the brunt of unpopular relations with Vichy France. But when it came to helping lay the groundwork for military landings in North Africa, State itself had a relatively insignificant part, being kept virtually uninformed on many important matters. It indeed provided an officer — Robert Murphy — to make the needed contacts, gather information and develop relationships but he was instructed by President Roosevelt to act not as a representative of State but as his personal agent, reporting directly and exclusively to the White House. State was left on the outside.

Not all of State's problems at this point were its own fault, but it was responsible for its basic weakness — its failure to keep abreast of the times, to perceive the basic trend of military diplomacy that had set in decades before, the moves of the military to prepare itself for greater and greater responsibilities and the corresponding need for the Department to move in the same direction and keep at least one step ahead.

The military at this juncture was not only comparatively well trained, well organized and alert, but also ably led. The War Department had George C. Marshall as Chief of Staff and Henry L. Stimson as its civilian Secretary. Both were seasoned in military and political affairs. Stimson, moreover, knew the diplomatic ropes. He had not only served as Secretary of War under President Taft and as a colonel in the 31st Artillery in World War I, but as Governor General of the Philippines and as Secretary of State under Herbert Hoover. If the Secretary of the Navy, Frank Knox, could not match such breadth of public service, he had proved in private business to be a hard negotiator and he worked with Stimson. Through the tangled web of wartime diplomacy the military moved under exceptionally able guidance.

When the shooting war ended, the military could not extricate itself from foreign affairs. The army inherited broad responsibilities for governing liberated areas, which comprised more land and a wider variety of cultures than it had governed at the end of the Spanish war. Some 200 million persons in areas as large and diverse as Germany, Austria, Trieste, Japan, Korea and the Ryukyu Islands, came under its rule. Law and order had to be maintained, relief distributed, economic life resumed. Education had to be purged of ultranationalistic and belligerent propaganda, free labor unions resurrected. Resources for democratic expression and leadership had to be mobilized, and public relations programs had to be devised for this purpose. All these tasks were directed toward the restoration of civilian government and an eventual restoration of peace through treaties and the evolution of democratic societies. As postwar developments show, the military establishment performed these complex tasks remarkably well. But equally significant for the purposes of our discussion was the training and experience which these responsibilities provided the military establishment, which emerged with a grasp of overseas affairs in some respects more extensive and detailed than that of our diplomatic establishment.

From the beginning of its occupation responsibilities — indeed in its wartime planning for these — the military asked not only for the diplomats' full cooperation, but also for as early a release from those responsibilities as possible. It insisted that State develop the policies to be applied in the occupied areas, and in August 1945 the President so ordered. A few months later, the military pressed for transfer of its occupation duties as well, but the Secretary of State demurred, arguing that his department was not prepared, and the proposal was dropped. Not until late 1949, when a West German Government of limited powers emerged, did German affairs seem sufficiently settled to be manageable by the diplomats. Even then, a military officer was posted in State to direct those affairs. A year later, a similar transfer of responsibility was effected with respect to Austria. Little by little, the military's occupation diplomacy came successfully to an end.

But the commingling of military and diplomatic affairs in

our foreign relations never terminated. While the authors of the United Nations had clearly foreseen the need for providing military support of UN diplomacy and had stipulated that a military committee exist within the organization, it was not this provision but Stalin's cold war thrust that assured the military of a continuing, large-scale involvement in international affairs. As one Central European country after another fell prey to Soviet subversion and violence, the free nations of the West saw their victory over dictatorship plucked from them country by country.

Redressment of the international balance would have come far more slowly had not a gifted military mind been summoned to head the State Department. The designation of General Marshall as head of the diplomatic establishment was one of those rare decisions which turn the tide of human events. A decisive President now had at his right hand an equally decisive Secretary of State, a broadly experienced man, a military professional with the instincts and vision of a civilian.

Marshall had hardly settled in his diplomatic assignment when his ability to develop rapidly the elements of a positive diplomacy was put to the test. The British warned of their imminent collapse in Greece and Turkey. Intervention by the United States was required and came decisively. Our assistance was as swiftly mobilized and dispatched as humanly possible. It covered virtually all areas of Greek society, and it went only slightly less far in Turkey.

In spite of this kind of rapid and decisive assistance our overall situation remained precarious. Hasty withdrawal of troops from abroad and demobilization at the end of World

War II had left us militarily exposed and the ambling habits of the State Department had left us diplomatically vulnerable. Even in our programs for Greece and Turkey, all did not go well: the embassies in Athens and Ankara were unprepared; the aid administrators dispatched from Washington were inadequately briefed. As late as February 1948 Marshall was uneasy over our performance. "We are playing with fire," he said, "while we have nothing with which to put it out," and he meant by this not only force but the whole range of diplomatic resourcefulness. He created a Policy Planning Staff in State and put it hard to work on large strategy and tactics. From it gradually emerged constructive, sharply focused proposals of diplomatic action. As Senator Vandenberg put it, "surrender days" were over and the new administration's determination "to get tough with Russia" was supplemented by bold, constructive measures of assistance to nations aspiring to freedom.

The Marshall Plan set in motion the economic reconstruction of Western Europe. A year after Marshall's complaint of insufficient means for fighting fires came the North Atlantic Treaty Organization (NATO). This set a pattern for the subsequent South East Asia Treaty Organization (SEATO) and the Central Treaty Organization (CENTO) in the Middle East. Supplementing these plural defense systems various trilateral and bilateral security pacts were developed to meet the needs of more limited areas under threat and to provide greater flexibility of negotiation and defense. All of these arrangements infused into our diplomacy a mixture of military, economic, political and social issues which heavily taxed our diplomatic capacity.

Two portentous developments in the latter months of 1949 brought further warning of the need for a more systematic fusion of military and diplomatic thinking. Even as the military establishment was transferring to State its administrative responsibilities in Germany and anticipating a similar move in Austria; even as we were handed a solution to the Greek civil war by Yugoslavia's defection from the Soviet bloc — which sealed off the Yugo-Greek border — the Soviets detonated their first nuclear device. A few months later the communists completed their mainland conquest of China. In November, at the thirty-second anniversary of their revolution, the Soviet leaders dramatized the new situation in an extraordinarily truculent expression of hostility toward the West and its sluggish development of military-diplomatic resources.

Now came a soul-searching in our government. We obviously had to take a hard look at things and it is interesting that, in a continuation of Marshall's leadership, the initiative came from State. Dean Acheson was now the Department's head. As Marshall's deputy, he had not only undergone a complete grounding in the diplomatic establishment but fully shared Marshall's emphasis upon research and planning in the development of State Department strategy. He and his planning associates pressed for a major review of the nation's military resources in relation to our increasing commitments to Free World defense. The National Security Council, which had by then come into existence, responded with an appropriate recommendation; the President concurred and in the ensuing general strategic reassessment State played a major part. The importance of military strategy and tactics had at last been recognized by the civilian summit of the diplomatic establishment. More than that, Marshall and Acheson had

culled from that establishment and brought in from the outside the needed talent to assume the responsibility of fusing
political with military leadership in foreign affairs.

State was ready to take the initiative in the matter of the
thermonuclear bomb, a device which, relying on fusion rather
than on fission, would unleash even greater explosive power in
an already unsteady world. It pressed for a general reconsideration of the bomb problem in the context of our general foreign policy. This involved the Atomic Energy Commission,
which State now significantly challenged for the first time.
The hesitations of the Commission head, David Lilienthal,
were overruled on January 30, 1950, by the President. Approv-
ing a directive drafted in the State Department, the Chief Executive authorized State and Defense to proceed to an overall
review of American foreign and defense policy in the context
of the loss of China, the Soviet mastery of atomic energy and
the prospect of an American fusion bomb.

It had now become evident that, as Masland and Radway
have put it, to "attain national security objectives without resort to war requires a national strategy in which the disposition of military forces is integrated with political bargaining,
policy statements, alliances, foreign economic policy, propaganda, and any and all measures" that may foster the growth
of friendly and cooperative minds within foreign governments.
Not only to limit the possibilities of war and the purposes and
scope of war, but to improve the well-being of peoples, the
closest cooperation between diplomatic and military establishments was demanded. This, in turn, required strong leadership by the State Department. Only the singular geniuses of
Marshall and Acheson produced it.

State's great hour of leadership in the military-diplomatic

area lasted until 1953. With the change in political administration, the Department lost not only brilliant members of its policy planning staff but much of its awareness of the importance of planning. The planner yielded ground to the prima donna; the strategist gave way to the improvising tactician. State never regained its initiative in politico-military affairs.

The Department now settled back to its customary practices. It continued to send a few of its officers each year to the various war colleges. It assigned diplomatic officers as faculty members at the war colleges, one to each. In 1960, at the prodding of Congress, it initiated an exchange of officers with the Pentagon. In addition, it rotated Foreign Service officers as political advisers to major military commanders.

But these measures, still carried out today, only touch upon the central problem: they do not grapple with it. And even such limited effect as they have has been diminished by the Department's slackness. Officers assigned to the war colleges, for instance, are very few in number, and they are rarely selected with any idea in mind of where and whether they will use their military knowledge. They are often chosen just because they happen to be around the Department and at loose ends. After completing a portion of their nine-to-ten-month course at war college, they can be seen in State trying to line up their next assignment, for the Department rarely shows an interest in their recent exposure to military affairs. Admittedly this exposure is brief and superficial, but it should nevertheless be used systematically. Since the officers' knowledge is not used, the officers themselves fail to concentrate to the end on learning all they can. By the middle of the course, they have to begin searching for their next job.

So, too, with the other procedures. Officers assigned as war college faculty members or as political "advisers" are provided no systematic preparation for these responsibilities. In addition, they often fail to bring much experience back with them to State. Indeed, faculty assignments have been given on occasion to officers in the process of being retired or to men who need an easy, leisurely year after a particularly strenuous assignment.

"Political advisers" to major military commanders are particularly ineffective, for they are not institutional representatives of State and hence not even liaison officers. They are very much on their own, and their positions are therefore not seriously responsible. They provide what State euphemistically calls "a specialized expertise" but what more accurately might be called — in view of the superficial preparation and training of diplomatic officers in diplomacy and international law — "a point of view." The Department claims to be "actively engaged in strengthening" the advisers' program, and to be trying "to upgrade qualitatively the personnel assigned to these jobs by selecting, through an exhaustive review process, officers with the stature, background, and experience which would enable them to function effectively as senior advisers to key commanders." This is the kind of language a bureaucracy employs to express wishful thinking. Not yet has it occurred to State that what is basically needed is not an "exhaustive" selection process but an exhaustive preparation and training process so that it has the kind of officers it needs "to function effectively as senior advisers to key commanders" and a subsequent placement process to take full advantage of the experience gained.

Apart from these personnel devices, a few organizational excursions into the politico-military area have occurred from time to time. During World War II, a State-War-Navy coordinating committee provided what has since become a familiar technique for fitting together some of the disparate pieces of the military-diplomatic jigsaw puzzle, and this kind of committee, now commonly called the "task force," is resorted to in crises. When Marshall and Acheson drove the planning wedge into the heart of the diplomatic establishment, and Marshall developed the real military expertise needed for leadership, State's Policy Planning Staff worked closely with the Joint Chiefs of Staff. But 1949-53 is a long time ago and the decline of State's military expertise has caused much of its leadership in this area to dissipate itself. While the National Security Council and a Senior Interdepartmental Group offer machinery for a high-level coordination of military-diplomatic elements in specific situations, coordination has to take place not just at the summit but all the way down to the country director in State. With the dismantlement of the Operations Coordinating Board this has been missing.

To take up some of its training and operating slack, the Department has tried to strengthen its top-level handling of politico-military matters. Military officers have been assigned to some of its geographic bureaus as advisers and, more recently, to its Policy Planning Staff. To organize disparate bits of operating activity and advice a staff was given to the Deputy Under Secretary for Political Affairs in May 1961, a few months after the termination of OCB. The Department had, indeed, long been pushed to provide one clear point of contact with the Pentagon, and with the decline of the Policy Planning

Staff from 1953 to 1961 a unit had been increasingly needed for this purpose, as well as for the purpose of encouraging a worldwide view of our politico-military problems. Accordingly, in 1961, sixteen years after the Second World War, twelve years after the formal beginning of the cold war, eleven years after the Defense Department had acted to meet a similar problem and eight years after the back of the Policy Planning Staff was broken, the State Department moved to provide this centralization of its politico-military operations.

Ignoring the fact that, in spite of all staff and organizational arrangements, decisions will still be made by officers, the Department continued to be little concerned with the training of diplomatic officers in military affairs. It consequently found that few of its personnel and none of its organizational tinkering enabled it to cope successfully with the complex military-political problems facing us as a World Power. As a result, it has clearly failed to provide the dynamic leadership which cold and hot wars have demanded. Let us consider how the military mind has moved to fill the serious gaps in our defense system left by these inadequacies.

Whatever its limitations, the military mind is a practical mind — systematic, alert, trained to examine every allied or hostile organization for weakness. It is also a mind used to careful staffing, to prescribing precisely who does what, and when, and where. While in the past, it has tended to prepare for yesterday's wars, today — under the compulsion of rapid scientific discoveries and by contrast with the diplomatic mind — it looks ahead. It thus, almost instinctively, moves in to fill the vacuums left by the State Department's inadequacies.

The military has been assisted in this by another of its attributes, that of thinking less frequently of political jurisdiction than do civilian agencies. It has its own inter-service rivalries, to be sure, but in its relations with the rest of the Federal establishment, professional education and training provide all the status and room for maneuver that it needs. It does not have to "get into the act"; there is hardly an area of foreign affairs that it is not already in and has not been in for a long time. It therefore thinks primarily in terms of the job to be done and how to get it done. This has helped to put the military's relations with the State Department on a practical, although highly competitive, basis.

A striking feature of the operations of the military establishment has helped it to be effective in its relationships with the diplomatic. To a remarkable degree, the military is involved in civilian society. Unlike the diplomats', the military's participation in foreign affairs carries with it a broadly based civilian relationship. This is not only operational in character: it is cultural, scientific, intellectual, political and industrial as well.

To begin with an obvious beginning, the military recruits civilians. It must test, judge, and train civilians. Moreover, it recruits from a broad spectrum of our society, including many who eventually wind up in the diplomatic establishment. Therefore, the tests and training that it must give these men rely heavily upon the psychological and psychiatric resources of the nation. These, in turn, bring it in closer touch with scholarly research on a broader basis than the State Department has ever been. In fact, many problems faced by the military have inspired academic experimentation with new techniques and new ideas, which in turn have led to increases in social-scientific knowledge.

This intellectual-academic relationship has been extended by other programs. The military establishment extensively subsidizes research — sociological as well as scientific — for the development of both ideas and weapons, and it has even created private corporations for these purposes. In addition, extensive programs of college education are provided for officers. The proportion of officers holding advanced degrees is so high it is not uncommon these days to find combat colonels holding the degree of doctor of philosophy.

Beyond these technical and academic relations, the military maintains many others with civilian life. The quartering, entertainment and religious counseling of servicemen, the education of their children, the enforcement of local laws, and just good public relations in general demand of every military base within the nation community relationships of a varied nature. Civilian advisory committees on these matters cluster around every military installation, drawing into their fold community leaders, clubwomen, labor representatives and even farmers. These committees, as the military say, are "members of our team . . . they give us active support and advice . . . they are asked for reactions to various phases of the Army's program. This involves study and thought on their part; as they become more indoctrinated themselves, they become our spokesmen."

These relationships extend upward, affecting such highly responsible functions as those of State government, the National Guard, our Civil Defense program, and the national educational-scientific-labor-industrial complex. All this induces considerable familiarity with labor organizations and collective bargaining. Finally, a sizable part of the personnel of the military establishment is civilian, providing a constant, persistent fertilization of the military mind in its daily policy-making.

The military establishment is thus more than a "military"

establishment. It is a vast, complicated social institution, of plural needs, of plural staffing, of plural relationships with the American society. The military not only identifies with that society from the grass roots up, but it also knows what makes the nation tick, its techniques of social action, its problems and pressures, its weaknesses and strengths. The diplomatic establishment does not remotely approach this degree of identification and understanding. Indicative of this has been the rise of military officers to the top civilian positions of the nation, including the Presidency and the headship of the State Department itself, while diplomats have signally failed to achieve any such breadth of national acceptance.

The far-reaching effects of this phenomenon include some psychological ones. Not only has a strong civilian mentality been engendered in the military, enabling it to deal successfully with civilian organizations like the State Department at home and governments abroad, but a spirit of inquiry has been fostered to challenge the military's discipline, sense of obedience and inclination to "fight the last war." A willingness to take extensive advantage of the research potential, both of this nation and of others, has developed, and use of military assistance programs for the purpose is symptomatic of this attitude.

All of this explains why a year in a military college deepens a diplomatic officer's "appreciation for the perception, range of knowledge, and sound common sense of the often maligned 'military mind.'" Indeed, one may question whether there is any longer "a military mind." The military establishment gives every indication, in fact, of having become a remarkable community of minds.

Unlike a diplomatic careerist, an able, ambitious military

officer can rise to the highest ranks of his profession in areas like research, intelligence, teaching, public relations, administration and supply. He can do so with satisfaction on his part and his combat colleagues' that such a contribution is as important as firing a gun. In line with this development, a general can become chairman of the Joint Chiefs of Staff without having had combat command in the field. This realistic attitude toward its great diversity of needs and its broad-ranged techniques of meeting such needs has enabled the military not only to manage its affairs more professionally than the diplomatic establishment, but to contribute perceptibly to overcoming inadequacies in diplomatic management itself.

An important corollary of all this must now be noted — the extent to which the military has grown into a negotiating establishment. At home and abroad it negotiates with producers of military supplies of all sorts. It negotiates with local citizens and communities. It participates in negotiations with national governments for foreign bases and, from base rights, negotiations spread like an oil slick over an impressive area. The very employment of foreign nationals at its far-ranging installations obliges the military to negotiate not only with them but their labor organizations, with local communities, and with national ministries of labor, welfare, finance, and sometimes foreign affairs.

Even more profoundly our military establishment has become involved in underdeveloped societies. Under the necessity of contributing to the training and equipping of military forces to prevent communist take-overs, our military strategists have developed a rather sophisticated concept of the military's role in the directing of the evolution of backward societies toward the democratic objectives of our general diplomacy. As a result, the philosophy and techniques of broad social development and negotiation which have been evolved at home and in advanced societies abroad, are now applied to this serious challenge.

"Civic action" programs have been brought to fruition to put the indigenous military forces to work helping peasants build schools, clinics, and roads to markets. In some areas, the indigenous military groups dispense medical treatment to the general population and organize civilian groups advisory to the military. They have thereby been brought face to face with the social problems of their peoples, taught a sense of social responsibility, and set on the road to discharging these responsibilities. Democratic attitudes have thus been encouraged. Reciprocally, these programs have reinforced within our own military establishment an awareness of the deep sociological forces which must be reckoned with in the world and given impetus to the increasing sophistication of that establishment's research and training efforts.

The traditional concept of the military establishment as simply an instrument of force and the diplomatic as an instrument of negotiation was never quite accurate and today is nonsensical folklore. That can be said also of the notion that the military takes over only when the diplomats fail.

The military's skill in performing a broad range of foreign-affairs functions and its greater ability to obtain funds for research and planning have enabled it to outpace the diplomatic establishment in many ways. This has created significant strains between the two. The Department — especially the career element in the pyramidal mass — has tried to overcome its disadvantage by recourse to smugness, to downgrading "the military mind" and military skill generally. This, in turn, increases the military's dissatisfaction over State's ambling, makeshift ways. Beneath the top leadership of the military establishment lies a hard substratum of discontent with the quality of our diplomacy and a widespread feeling that State has a "no win" inadequacy. When the two establishments are brought into close operating relationships in complex situations, as in Vietnam today, Greece or Berlin, Lebanon and the Congo yesterday, and where-you-will tomorrow, comparisons of their differences in experience, skills and capacities inevitably are made, and Presidents often find themselves giving greater weight to military than to diplomatic advice, dispatching military officers as ambassadors and sending Secretaries of Defense alone rather than in the company of Secretaries of State to trouble-spots for analyses and proposals of what to do next. This bodes ill for the diplomatic establishment and for our kind of society in the hard years ahead. But State seems no more alive to this profound danger than to others. As long as it enjoys passably amicable relationships with the military it considers its job done, just as it too often considers its job done abroad if it can only enjoy amicable relationships with other governments. Its challenge is far deeper than that.

CHAPTER 6

Of Secret Operations
and Much Confusion

THE RELATIONS of the State Department with the Central Intelligence Agency are of the most critical sort. They influence the Department's effectiveness, our Government's overall management of foreign affairs, and the moral and political principles which we claim to stand for at home and abroad. They are thus crucial to all phases of the leadership we try to exercise in world affairs.

Section 102 (d) of the National Security Act of 1947 which established the CIA provides that the Agency "correlate and evaluate intelligence relating to the national security, and provide for the appropriate dissemination of such intelligence within the Government, using where appropriate existing agencies and facilities." This is a clear statement — as long as one knows what "intelligence" is.

"Intelligence" is simply evaluated information. If we know that a man has landed on the coast of Cuba with a handful of guerrillas and begun hostile operations against the Cuban Government, we have information. Intelligence, on the other hand, tells us who he and his associates are, in terms of background, psychological makeup, and political philosophy; what their objectives and chances of success are, and what the results of their success or failure may be.

The CIA is not alone in gathering information pertinent to national defense and converting it into intelligence. It was not intended by the National Security Act to monopolize these functions. Nor has it attempted to do so. It specializes in collecting information by surreptitious means, acting as a clearinghouse for all intelligence and assisting the other members of the intelligence community (primarily State, Defense, the Atomic Energy Commission, and the FBI) with some of their special assignments.

Governments — our own included — have from time immemorial engaged in spying. Whenever we have been faced with a serious problem of gaining or preserving our independence we have resorted to espionage and much that goes with it, including the bribery of foreign officials. We have not liked it. It has always been repugnant to us. But we, like everyone else, have had to yield to the dictates of necessity.

It was our good fortune for many years to have little or no need of espionage in our overseas diplomacy. We used it against the Indians at home, for this was a matter of survival, but once our independence was assured we could give it up in overseas dealings, and it is to our credit that we did so. Our moral compunctions made it hard even for seasoned diplomats to learn the facts about our changing position as we moved into international politics, however, and World War I found us at a considerable disadvantage.

A perfect illustration of our dilemma began to unfold in 1913 when one Herbert O. Yardley joined the State Department as a young code clerk. Imaginative, questioning, ingenious, he began to suspect that the Department's code system was unsafe against the intelligence activities of other governments. To test the soundness of his suspicions he applied himself to breaking all the Department's codes without reference to any key. He succeeded. He could not get his point across to the diplomats, however, and, finally discouraged, approached the military intelligence division of the War Department with a proposal to develop a cryptographic unit for breaking codes and devising safe ones.

The War Department took Yardley on, and, while his discouragement by no means ended, he was eventually authorized to organize MI-8, the Intelligence Corps' first unit to invent new military codes and crack those of other governments. The value of his work became apparent when Yardley deciphered a long message of the German Government offering a generous reward to Mexico for remaining neutral in World War I.

After the reestablishment of peace, the War Department and State arranged to support a group of skilled cryptographers with Yardley at its head. Although he knew not a word of the Japanese language, Yardley was able to crack the Japanese code during preparations for the 1922 Washington Disarmament Conference. The United States Government therefore knew precisely what the various fall-back positions of the Japanese delegation were to be and bargained accordingly. The diplomatic advantage of such feats was immeasurable, for we had little preparation to buttress our ambition to exercise some influence in postwar international affairs. By 1929, Yardley and the little group which he had trained had broken the codes of some twenty countries, including those of Britain, France, the Soviet Union and Japan. They thereby kept State posted on transactions and decisions of foreign governments as no diplomatic officers could possibly have done.

The climax to this revealing piece of history came in 1929, when Henry L. Stimson became Secretary of State. As we have already had occasion to note, Stimson was a man seasoned in public and military affairs. But peacetime intelligence was something else. A few days after taking charge of State, he found on his desk several deciphered messages of a diplomatic mission in Washington. Demanding to know where and how such materials had originated, he was apprised of Yardley's operation. Stimson ordered immediate cessation of State's support. "Gentlemen," he as much as said, "do not read each other's mail."

The difficulty was, not everybody engaging in international affairs was a gentleman. There were those who did read others' mail and based their diplomatic moves accordingly. Naïve though he was in this matter, Stimson had his way. With funds cut off, Yardley had to disband his staff. But before retiring to write a bitter, fascinating book on his disillusioning experience, he spoke his mind. In a final interview with a State Department official, he repeated that every one of the Department's codes could be, and probably had been, broken by foreign governments, just as he had broken theirs. While he had been developing safe codes for the military, no one had been doing this for State. "Your codes," he said bluntly, "are just as cumbersome, just as antiquated as sixteenth-century communications."

The uneasy official asked what could be done. Yardley

pointed out that machines on the market could be adapted to eliminate all possibilities of cracking. The ominous warning was as clear as a bell — and the solution too — but nothing was done about it.

The Department — and the government — were to pay heavily. As World War II approached, our efforts to meet its challenges engaged us in all sorts of activity designed not only to assure supplies of strategic materials — rubber, tin, oil and the like — but to stockpile these against the possibility of war. When war came, we used our period of neutrality to sap the power of governments clearly hostile to us by bidding against them for these materials and wangling higher priority for our orders than we were entitled to. It was no time to be squeamish. We matched chicanery with chicanery. This was done through a specially created agency.

The greater such activities became, the greater became our need of information — a more systematic, thorough collection, a more rapid collection, a more accurate evaluation, a more effective distribution to all departments and agencies concerned with our growing effort of survival. The interest and initiative of State in all this were far below requirements and it was from outside the diplomatic establishment that the urgency of the task was brought to the President's attention. Aware of the deficiencies of State and the military, and realizing the imperative need for a larger, more professional, less orthodox effort, a New York lawyer and Republican leader of military experience went to Washington in 1940 and laid the problem squarely before the White House. Col. William J. Donovan soon found himself on a rapid investigation trip to Europe at the end of which he was made head of an "Office of the Coordinator of Information," directly responsible to the President. Later, when this organization was split into the Office of War Information and the Office of Strategic Services, Donovan, heading the latter, was still answerable only to the White House. State was bypassed.

At the same time that Donovan and Roosevelt discussed the critical need for more and prompter information, they reviewed another of Donovan's ideas — the combining of intelligence with support of resistance movements and (if we should become involved in war, as then seemed probable) the harassment of the enemy by guerilla forces. When war came and the Office of Strategic Services crystallized out of the OCI, this dangerous, semi-military operation was rapidly set in motion.

We must pass over the colorful history of OSS but we should have clearly in mind what it was designed to do, for it led directly to the Central Intelligence Agency. It had five functions: (1) to gather information all over the world by any and all means, open and clandestine, including underground activities in harassment of the enemy; (2) to process all this information, turning it into intelligence; (3) to pass this intelligence on to interested components of the government; (4) to receive, process and distribute intelligence from other government agencies and from foreign governments; (5) to wound the enemy by all possible means short of conventional military operations.

Hastily improvised, the OSS made its share of mistakes. Considering the difficulties, however, Donovan and his associates did an extraordinary job. A factor essential for their success was their insistence upon the meticulous training of their operators. They were able to provide this training because of an arrangement with the military establishment. State could have done this, too, in order better to qualify its own people. But this never occurred to State. Nor has it occurred since.

Like the military, OSS was an action agency. The mass of information it assembled was designed to achieve specific results. Research and investigation were directly related to those results. In other words, the operators carried out what the researchers, strategists and tacticians had decided could and should be done, taking into account the known circumstances.

When World War II came to an end, the need for centralizing so fundamental an activity as intelligence was widely recognized, and a move was made to give the responsibility to State. The Bureau of the Budget so recommended and President Truman, in abolishing the OSS in the fall of 1945, transferred its saboteurs to the military establishment and its experienced intelligence analysts to the diplomatic, notifying the Secretary of State:

> I particularly desire that you take the lead in developing a comprehensive and coordinated foreign intelligence program for all Federal agencies concerned with that type of activity. This should be done through the creation of an interdepartmental group, heading up under the State Department.

The President, like the Budget Bureau, overestimated the capacity of State. Had it been simply a matter of creating "an interdepartmental group," State might have muddled through. But the problem was more than organizational and certainly involved more than adding another inter-agency committee to the Federal apparatus.

State went through the motions of carrying out the President's directive. A special assistant to the Secretary was appointed to deal with research and intelligence. An interdepartmental group was created, as directed. Space was found for some 1600 persons, including a large number of former OSS staffers. Then the effort tapered off. State could not muster the imagination to use its new resources properly. It could not even provide a hospitable environment. Its diplomatic officers were not about to surrender their old status. They wanted their old center of power to continue in the geographic bureaus. The old fraternity sensibilities came into play. The old resistance to new ideas. The old smugness.

One by one OSS staff members dropped away. Dissatisfaction spread in the government's intelligence community. The President stepped in, reversed his earlier order and established an Intelligence Authority independent of State. The operating arm of this Authority was a newly-formed Central Intelligence Group which a year later became the Central Intelligence Agency, under a director subject to the supervision of the National Security Council. State's removal from the centralizing and coordinating role was thus effected.

So CIA at its birth was something more than a rival of State. It was more than another agency with an "itch to get into the act." It was an agency whose very existence attested to the incompetence of the diplomatic establishment.

CIA now got its own intelligence gatherers — i.e., spies — into each of our missions abroad. They worked independently of the rest of the mission staff. They reported to their headquarters in Washington in their own code, as a foreign government would do. They played their cards close to their vest. Their diplomatic colleagues in the missions to which they were attached rarely knew what information they were ferreting out. Even the ambassador seldom knew — he who was supposed to be in charge of and responsible for all a mission's activities. CIA was in many ways a secret intelligence operation even with respect to its own government.

These factors introduced a serious psychological problem. They meant that every piece of information CIA got and State didn't was a reflection upon State, a reflection on the efficacy of its diplomatic officers and their awareness of what was going on. It was a CIA "scoop" and it rankled. It made the diplomats want to downgrade or ignore some of CIA's more alarming news, particularly if it did not corroborate their own. This made difficult not only State-CIA relations but the whole process of putting information and intelligence to accurate and constructive use. The kind of tightly-knit intelligence operation needed for our success just was not there. Nor is it today.

It would have done no good to have reminded State that the independence of CIA was due to its own failure. But it might have done some good if State had recognized that there was not only an organizational but a psychological problem in all this: since State had made life miserable for the intelligence officers inherited from OSS, the latter, when transferred to CIA and released from their humiliations in State, rejoiced in the opportunity of thumbing their noses at their erstwhile colleagues. For if State had only seen this aspect of the problem, it could have moved to train its officers to cope with it; once involved with training of that limited sort, it quite possibly might have gone on to deal with other factors, such as its own careless security arrangements, which also were properly viewed with concern by the CIA. But at no point did all this dawn on State.

We come now to a most sensitive item, one that accounts for great, and often serious confusion in our foreign affairs. The National Security Act, in addition to delegating the intelligence function to CIA, authorized it "to perform, for the benefit of the existing intelligence agencies, such additional services of common concern as the National Security Council determines can be most efficiently accomplished centrally." This, if language means anything, authorized CIA to engage in intelligence activities additional to those spelled out in the Act — the additional activities to be for the benefit of "the existing intelligence agencies." But the Act did not mean that, and wasn't intended to. What the language was intended to cover up was the kind of subversive activity, promotion of guerilla warfare and the like, which OSS had engaged in and which the National Security Council might decide in a particular situation was necessary for the defense of our interests.

To conduct its "special operations," CIA set up a Plans Division and hired Allen Dulles, a former OSS operator, to be its first director. This was under President Truman — an interesting point, as we shall see. With the imaginativeness and boldness demonstrated in their earlier OSS operations, Dulles and his associates were off to new ventures and it became clear that some stronger control was needed than that supplied by the National Security Council, whose members met infrequently and hurriedly and dispersed to pressing duties in their respective departments. A "Special Group" evolved, consisting of the Director of the CIA, the Under Secretary of State for Political Affairs and representatives of the military establishment. The Group came late on the scene. It grew out of an "OCB luncheon group," which itself came sometime after CIA had got a head start on its secret operations, and thus it inherited a rather casual character.

Meeting about once a week, the group carries on its discussions informally, a fact which is an asset to CIA's secrecy, since it enables the Agency not only to control the agenda but also to steer discussion away from matters it prefers the others not to know about. And since CIA's representative presides over the Group, it can seize the initiative at the outset of a meeting and consume the entire session with a prickly question unrelated to more dubious activities. Moreover, the CIA representative is a Presidential appointee. The State Department member has found it hard to probe deeply, much less to steer or contest, the work of a Presidential appointee directing an autonomous Agency. He just doesn't have that status. Moreover (and here we touch a vital point), he is generally a rotated officer. He cannot match the inside knowledge, the political prestige and the weight of continuous experience which the CIA Director can muster. Because of the failure of State to dominate the Group, the theory that the latter should inform all interested establishments of what CIA is doing, and that all CIA activities should be carried on within the framework of foreign policies set by State, does not work out in practice. This has been amply publicized by politically appointed ambassadors and the press. State is kept in the dark about many CIA operations abroad and especially about those which run counter to the Department's policies.

Somewhere along the line, State should have seen the handwriting on the wall, so visible to others, and moved to train its own officers to lead and control in this area. It should have strengthened the OCB, which held promise of developing Federal plans and disciplines. But in its fluctuating, fragmentary way, with personnel in today and gone tomorrow, it only grumbled about CIA. Its rotating officers never took time to ask themselves what the Agency operations portended for State and the government; never studied the functions and training methods of the Agency; never sought to bring the training of its own officers up to a level competitive with CIA so as to reduce the need of the Agency's unorthodox activities.

Living with CIA has thus become more and more difficult. The Agency supported Indonesian rebels against Sukarno while State was trying to work with Sukarno. It supplied and emboldened the anticommunist Chinese guerillas in Burma over the protests of the Burmese Government and the repeated protestations of the State Department in Washington and our ambassador in Burma that we were doing no such thing. In Vietnam, too, CIA and State have worked at cross-purposes.

But the Agency has not confined its activities to unstable countries. It has meddled elsewhere, to the consternation of the State Department and friendly governments. In the mid-1950s, its agents intruded awkwardly in Costa Rica, the most stable and democratic country in Latin America. While the Agency was trying to oust Jose Figueres, the moderate socialist who became the Costa Rican President in a fair election in 1953, the State Department was working with him and our ambassador was urging President Eisenhower to invite him to the United States to enhance his prestige. So it went the world around.

It was the CIA that negotiated with the Guatemalan Government for the right and facilities to train Cuban refugees to invade their country. It paid the refugees, trained them, arranged for their transportation to the Bay of Pigs, where they sought to overthrow the Castro regime by force of arms supplied by CIA. It was the CIA, and the Joint Chiefs of Staff, which assured two Presidents the venture was feasible. The State Department hardly knew what was going on. It could not seriously analyze or contest the project.

CIA thus has done everything, as part of its "special operations," from peaceful frustration of communists to peaceful frustration of the State Department; from deciding whom we would back among various possibilities in a given country to undercutting people the State Department backs, and on to fomenting and conducting undeclared wars. Little by little it has moved into an area of decision and action reserved by the Constitution for the President alone, spreading contradictions and confusion in our foreign policies along the way.

It has been enough to awe ex-President Truman, who soon began to have the gravest misgivings about the agency he had created. He wrote in a syndicated newspaper article in late 1953:

> With all the nonsense put out by Communist propaganda . . . in their name-calling assault on the West, the last thing we needed was for the CIA to be seized upon as something akin to a subverting influence in the affairs of other people. . . .
>
> There are now some searching questions that need to be answered. I . . . would like to see the CIA restored to its original assignment as the intelligence arm of the President, and whatever else it can properly perform in that special field — and that its operational duties be terminated or properly used elsewhere.

We have grown up as a nation, respected for our free institutions and for our ability to maintain a free and open society.
There is something about the way the CIA has been functioning that is casting a shadow over our historic position and I
feel that we need to correct it.

It may be that Mr. Truman as President was not fully
aware, when he signed the order establishing the CIA, that he
was subscribing to language which carried CIA beyond the intelligence area. He may not have been aware that a Plans Division, to conduct CIA's special operations, was established in
1951 under his Presidency. He may not have known that Allen
Dulles came to Washington to be the first director of that
division during Mr. Truman's occupancy of the White House.
Presidents are busy officials. They cannot keep up with everything. They must go a good deal on what their associates tell,
or don't tell, them. But by the close of 1953 Mr. Truman was
alarmed by the magnitude of CIA operations and by the basic
issues these operations were presenting not only to our Federal
Government and to friendly foreign governments but to the
form of our society. This was also enough to worry the State
Department and many a thoughtful citizen.

"Today," Allen W. Dulles has observed, "the Soviet State
Security Service (KGB) is the eyes and ears of the Soviet
State abroad, as well as at home. It is a multi-purpose, clandestine arm of power that can in the last analysis carry out
almost any act that the Soviet leadership assigns to it. It is
more than a secret police organization, more than an intelligence and counter-intelligence organization. It is an instrument for subversion, manipulation and violence, for secret intervention in the affairs of other countries. It is an aggressive
arm of Soviet ambitions in the Cold War." The CIA may not

be a secret police organization but in every other respect it meets Mr. Dulles' description of the KGB. Through its independent agents, who are on the staffs of every one of our diplomatic missions and who report and act secretly, without informing the rest of the mission, including the ambassador, it provides our Government eyes and ears abroad. It is also an arm of our Government, a multi-purpose, clandestine arm of power. It is more than an intelligence organization. It is an instrument for secret intervention in the affairs of other countries, even to the point of waging undeclared war. It can be an aggressive arm. It is an untamed arm. Not only does it challenge the political principles and philosophy on which our government was founded: it challenges the clear language of the Constitution itself.

It has been pointed out that the State Department works very much on its own, regardless of who is Secretary of State or President. The CIA is also on its own, only very much more so. While State has secrets, it nevertheless operates as an open rather than a clandestine organization. It is not required, as are other departments and agencies of the government to submit an annual report to Congress, but it must submit annually a request for appropriations and answer questions about its request in public sessions of Congressional subcommittees. Its representatives must testify frequently before a variety of Congressional committees, hold press conferences, make speeches explaining what the Department is doing, and generally preserve an open, above-board operation.

None of this is true of CIA. Its budget is buried in the Defense Department budget. No one save a few CIA officials and the Comptroller of the Pentagon knows where it is hidden and how much it amounts to. No one even knows how large a staff CIA has. No one knows CIA's methods of personnel operations, so that, as Congressmen have often observed, no one really knows "whether we have a fine intelligence service or a very poor one." And Senator Mansfield has commented, "Secrecy beclouds everything about the CIA — its cost, its efficiency, its successes and its failures." CIA has so far evaded any close checking by Congress. The Armed Services and Appropriations Committees of both Houses do have subcommittees on the CIA but, like the executive "watchdog" apparatus, they never get below the surface of CIA affairs.

In this crucial area, the State Department cannot meet the situation with its present attitudes of mind, its present operating procedures, and its present inadequate training of officers. Its deficiencies oblige State to deal with CIA as though it were a foreign government, able to extract from it only as much information concerning its activities and only as much compliance with our general policy lines as CIA is willing, gratuitously, to grant — and it is not willing to grant enough. This is an impossible situation. But it will not be rectified until State places itself in a position to operate effectively and command respect because of its greater competence.

CHAPTER 7

The Front Line

To TRANSACT its overseas business, the State Department uses the Foreign Service of the United States. Under law, this is the Foreign Service of *the United States* and therefore of the entire government. In practice, it has acted as a field division of State. The relations of the two provide many of the reasons why our government as a whole often has such difficulty in winning understanding, respect and a following abroad.

The State Department accomplishes some of its aims through foreign ambassadors in Washington. Others it pursues through: (1) the United Nations; (2) regional organizations such as the OAS; (3) commodity arrangements such as the International Sugar Council and International Coffee Organization; (4) defense, scientific, and cultural unions, as well as a host of private instrumentalities. But the basis for much of the cooperation it seeks from foreign authorities is patiently built up by American representatives called Foreign Service officers, stationed in cities, towns and villages abroad. They do the work of accumulating stores of mutual understanding, respect, and willingness to cooperate. Negotiators at international conferences are rarely aware of how much they draw upon these reserves, since their attention is focused on the immediate bargaining points. Still less is the general public aware of the vast silent contribution of the Foreign Service.

One of the basic functions which the Service performs is the protection of the lives, property and interests of American citizens. This is not so unrelated to politics and policy as is sometimes believed. Nor is it to be confused with "dollar diplomacy." The function grows out of the ancient obligation of governments to honor the rights of each other's citizens, an obligation which evolved into one of the elementary principles of international law. The function has political importance, because any civilized government must perform it in order to command respect from others. As demonstrated all too often, a hostile government can discredit another nation simply by abusing its citizens. The implication that the other nation is too weak to protect its citizens while on foreign soil discredits the nation itself, undermines its prestige, and saps the vitality of its influence.

Obviously important for the successful exercise of this function (in an age when gunboat diplomacy can rarely be used), is a thorough training of our overseas representatives in international law, in the treaties which refine this law into specific obligations, in the techniques of peaceful enforcement, and in the psychologies, motivations, objectives and techniques of other governments and peoples. Equally important (in an age when newly independent and immature nations are numerous) is a thorough training in the diplomacy of protection. For we must keep in mind the fact that protection is something which must be gained in the environments of other societies, other cultures, and therefore demands an acute knowledge of not only rights and techniques but the psychologies, values and social customs of others.

The protection of citizens abroad is entrusted primarily to consular officers, located in sections of every embassy as well as in separate consular posts placed in the more important centers of population and trade. Because embassies are located only in capitals, consular posts are often nearer the scene of a given problem; but when ministries of foreign affairs must be appealed to, the embassies intervene.

Encouragement of American commerce is another function of the overseas posts. While this is of particular significance when our overseas trade earns less than the amount of our overseas expenditures and the nation is confronted by a "dollar gap" which drains our gold abroad, the promotion of American products and services must be continuous; the counteraction of discriminating tariffs and practices must go on, week in and week out. Since these efforts are directly related to our economic position in the world, they significantly influence our national defense. They are among the most vital — and least dramatized — duties of the "front line."

Consular posts are thus not as unrelated to national defense as is believed by many people — including improperly prepared Foreign Service officers who have traditionally disdained consular assignments. Such posts contribute — or can contribute if staffed by imaginative men — to virtually every function performed by embassies. Indeed, some report directly to Washington and receive their instructions from Washington, just like embassies. Some exercise their functions in areas more extensive than do many embassies, as in

India, where consular districts are larger than many European, Latin American and African countries. The importance of such posts is sizable, even though they are under the general supervision of an embassy.

The protective and trade promotion functions are sometimes closely related and can present delicate questions of diplomacy. What does one do, for example, about the contract that a political exile of a foreign country negotiates by sleight of hand between a department of his government and an American construction company for laying an oil pipeline when the head of that government discovers the sleight of hand and refuses to honor the agreement?

The company has acted in good faith, but not with good sense; it has no representative in the foreign country and has sent no special emissary there to check up on things. Its appeal to the State Department for assistance results in the Department dispatching a message to our embassy to corroborate the facts. Then the embassy talks over the matter with the foreign government, which continues adamant. When the Department advises the company to exhaust its capabilities of self-help by sending a representative to the country to talk directly with the government, the company explodes: "What kind of a State Department is this?" It goes to "the Hill" to solicit support from Congressmen to whom the Department is called upon to explain the situation. If the company winds up in the hands of a private consulting firm it will probably get the advice I know one such company received: "Get yourself a representative in that country and stop acting like an adolescent." Such a representative then works quietly with the foreign government, with such advice and assistance from our embassy as the situation permits. All the while, if Department and embassy are doing their job properly, each is keeping the other informed of developments and exchanging views as to what each might do.

In such a situation, an embassy is by no means simply an agent of the Department. It knows better than the Department the local situation and the possibilities for remedial action. On one occasion, our diplomatic representative in Managua received instructions from the Department to call on the President of Nicaragua and ask him to pay promptly a bill his Government owed a large American company. The diplomat — a political appointee — reminded the Secretary of State his mission was not the collection of private debts and he did not propose to approach anyone in the Nicaraguan Government on the matter. He heard no further from Washington. Our overseas representatives are not mere messenger boys — if they are doing their job.

Closely related to these functions are others, equally basic. One is constant probing of public and governmental opinion in countries abroad. Obviously, this is something that cannot be done in Washington, through the foreign ambassadors. It must be done by our own people, who know our interests and can seek information relevant to them. Our posts abroad are analogous to the reconnaissance parties of an army, advanced to explore the contours of the territory in which it must operate, to spot power centers and evaluate their strength, detect sources of hostility, friendship and indifference, ascertain ways in which resistance or indifference can be overcome and such support as may exist be reinforced and extended.

If done adequately, this continuous diplomatic and consular reconnaissance detects and deals with crises in their incipient stages; it discovers sources of antagonism and demagoguery, and treats them as promptly and fully as human ingenuity will permit. An overseas service can do this systematically, for each country, locality, political party, social group, leader and demagogue. In some countries, special emphasis is required for one particular set of groups, whether labor unions, universities, religions, ethnic groups, or tribes. In not a few countries, family connections and rivalries must be understood. Without such detailed knowledge, wrong approaches are made, *faux pas* committed which frustrate our objectives. Here is where the front line plays a crucial if subtle role in all we try to do, determining the degree to which our views and policies are respected.

Both the size and intricacy of this task arise from the fact that diplomacy is no longer limited to kings, aristocrats, politicians and industrialists, or to the societies of capitals. It is a composite — often a highly explosive one — of the multiple interests of whole nations — fishermen and physicians as well as financiers, bricklayers as well as bankers, peons as well as publishers. Therefore, the effective diplomatic officer is not the gentleman in cutaway coat and striped pants, whose most effective pose is on the day he presents his credentials, or lays a wreath, presides over an impressive desk flanked by the flag of the United States, attends an official function, makes a speech, or relays a local government's call for troops to forestall chaos. He is the man who travels extensively around the country to which he is posted, rubs shoulders with all sorts of men, comes to understand their needs and aspirations, detects their weaknesses, and contributes his bit of influence when our interest is at stake. This demands a sustained and profound understanding of a people and a society which cannot be gained in a couple of years. Nor is it to be gained in what Livingston Merchant has aptly called the "incestuous diplomatic foreign office group which you tend to find in any capital." The content of diplomacy these days is the stuff of human society itself — it is just that complex — and the most refined techniques of analysis and influence must be used to cope with it.

Entire continents brood with uncertainty. Peoples long wed to primitive cultures are seeking a viable adjustment to the modern world. Their problems are not simply political and economic — as we tend to think — but social, psychological, and spiritual as well. While we generously offer a certain amount of political tutelage and economic assistance, the hearts and minds of these people grope for something more. The focus of any civilization is not a hall of parliament or a locomotive or even a schoolhouse or a clinic: it is man. Of all the challenges our diplomatic establishment faces therefore, that of *man* and his needs is the greatest. Our diplomatic representatives must understand him in all his variety and this demands a depth of learning and comprehension never before required of them.

International relations and thus foreign policies generally proceed not directly but elliptically. For societies and their relationships are full of silences, full of unspoken assumptions, full of unarticulated psychologies. It is the task of diplomatic and consular officers to discover these assumptions and psychologies, to fill in these ellipses with their own understanding, their own interpretations, their own discoveries. The success of policy formulation and execution rests upon the skill with which this is done and this in turn depends upon the extensiveness and depth of learning, the intuitive genius and the training in techniques of social inquiry of these representatives all over the world. This is one of the reasons their education and training are so important.

Every overseas post is, thus, a relay station, picking up and passing along to Washington insights into peoples and their needs with suggestions of what, if anything, is to be done. This task must be performed for a Washington that functions thousands of miles away, in a wholly different environment. In such circumstances an overseas officer's communication with his own government is one of his more serious problems. *How* to cast reports and recommendations so as to sound convincing can be as tough a job as finding out *what* to report and recommend.

On the other hand, explanation of our own country — its social characteristics and problems, its policies at home and abroad, its diplomatic moves — is equally difficult, for differences in environment again interpose serious obstacles. How does one explain *our* society and policies to a Moslem or a Hindu, to a primitive African or indeed to a European or Latin American society of different cultural values? This demands a high degree of sophistication. Foreigners will detect a poor performance of this function by our diplomats, even when we do not.

It is not enough to create reservoirs of mutual understanding. The "front line" must contrive to encourage leaders, in and out of government, to draw upon them. Time and again we find ourselves taking a position or making a move which leaders of other governments privately tell us they agree with but cannot publicly support. Our overseas posts must go as far as the best brains, personalities, trained skills and resources of our nation can carry them in creating a favorable climate for our policies.

The continuing ferment of Panamanian hostility to our canal rights is a painful case in point. If we had had enough mature and sophisticated officers dealing with our Panamanian relations, undistracted by too frequent rotation, we might not have been exposed to so much obloquy and received so little public acknowledgement of the good we have done in constructing and operating a canal for the benefit of all. A sufficient number of good officers could have done the job — one that admittedly would not have been easy. Indeed, it would have required taking the lead from reactionaries on our side and demagogues on the other by means of a long-ranged plan and tactics, including sustained educational effort among Panamanians, the Americans living in the Canal Zone, and among officers in our military establishment and Congressmen. This would have required political ingenuity and guts, with the closest kind of coordination between the Department, the President, progressive Congressmen, the Defense Department, our ambassadors to Panama, our military governor of the Canal Zone and our Caribbean military commander, and the American residents of the Zone. This is what leadership means. But no such basic strategy was ever devised. No such sustained ingenuity and guts were brought to bear on the festering problem. And when Joseph S. Farland came along and showed himself to be superbly qualified to make an effective contribution, we used him a short while and then let him go.

Of course, if our posts abroad are to be not only vigorous but persuasive, they must avoid the impression of meddling. As anyone knows, advice, even to a friend, is one of the hardest things to give successfully. It can easily misfire and the giver find himself on the receiving end. Let me suggest by a couple of examples how the dilemma has been solved.

At a critical time in the history of Mexico, early in this century, David Eugene Thompson of Nebraska was our representative there. He was described by an American diplomatic officer who served with him as "a man of powerful personality, of large intelligence and shrewd judgment, and of sharp and forthright tongue. . . . By the lifelong exercise of a naturally strong intellect on a vast number and wide variety of books, he had, for all his lack of formal schooling, made himself into an unusually well-educated man. . . . His great value to his country lay in the fact that he possessed, as probably no other man possessed, the absolute confidence of the aging Mexican dictator, Don Porfirio Diaz . . . and the friendship between them illustrates the great and beneficent power a North American diplomat could, if he were trusted and well liked, exercise unofficially in Spanish American capitals." Now observe what this produced: "Aware of the relationship between the President and the Ambassador, state Governors, generals, police officials, federal judges and even judges of the supreme court would drop into the Embassy to consult him about any case that might happen to involve Americans or American interests." Here is leadership — indirectly exercised — but effective all the same because it was leadership sought, not imposed, and carried no taint of intervention.

Let us take another example, involving no dictatorship, and

this time in reverse — a foreign representative's influence with our own government. Consider Jules Jusserand, the French ambassador in Washington for thirteen years, from 1903 to 1915. Note, first, the length of service. Note, too, that Jusserand had published in 1889 *English Wayfaring Life in the Middle Ages*, six years later a *Literary History of the English People* and in 1898 *Shakespeare in France*. If the reader is inclined to question the relevance of English wayfaring life in the middle ages or literature or even history in general to diplomacy in the twentieth century, he may be betraying how little he knows of the subtleties of diplomatic leadership. And if he wonders how, today, a diplomatic officer of ours could engage in such pursuits, he may be raising one of the vital questions concerning the quality of our diplomacy and our problems of world leadership which the State Department itself, and Congress, have neglected to face.

Along with his considerable learning and his meditative turn of mind, Jusserand was tactful and analytical, practical and politically perceptive. And to what did such a combination of qualities lead? He became a close friend and adviser of an American President, one generally supposed so ebullient and self-confident as not to be in the market for much advice, especially from a foreigner. But when Theodore Roosevelt had a particularly difficult question to resolve, whether domestic or international, he came to seek the counsel of Jusserand. When Secretary of State John Hay was ill and the President wanted the best advice he could get, he turned not to the Number Two man in the State Department, nor to a member of his Cabinet, but to this learned, perceptive emissary of France. Remarkable was this relationship and it could not have evolved from any step of the French Government save the appointment of Jusserand as ambassador in Washington. Such influence could not have been exerted in Paris either by the President of France, her Premier or her Ministry of Foreign Affairs. It could only be developed in the overseas capital and even then it could come only from the knowledge, perceptiveness and personality of the emissary.

These conditions govern our own efforts to lead. No pontification from Washington can alone produce leadership. No mere parade of economic or military power can do it. It must come in large part from the personal qualifications of our diplomatic representatives throughout the world.

After an extensive trip through Asia, Robert Kennedy spoke of the results of our diplomacy in that area: "I found we have not yet made our position clear in a forceful way, partly because many of those who have gone abroad did not know the answers themselves." He went on: "While, out of courtesy, some government officials of foreign countries may not press for answers, the people of these nations want and expect and, in fact, should have our position lucidly explained." Of course this is true, and as we have noted, it is one of the most important functions of our Foreign Service but the diplomatic establishment has limped along for years doing a wholly inadequate job in these respects. The Foreign Service does not always possess even adequate contact with the peoples of other countries. I recall that one career officer who served in European countries where socialist and labor parties were important, rose to the rank of ambassador in one of them and boasted that he had never met a socialist or labor leader and never intended to. These social — or sociological — limitations assert themselves too often. Some acute observers felt they detected them in 1965 on the part of our embassy in the Dominican Republic. It took the Department years to designate Foreign Service officers as "provincial reporters" and set them roaming through Vietnam to keep us passably well informed of that troubled country and assist in keeping the Vietnamese people in touch with us.

The Department, in operating practices, often handicaps and obstructs the kind of front-line initiative on which our world leadership depends. Henry S. Villard, a career officer of the Foreign Service, tells the following story of what occurred when he was our ambassador to Libya a few years ago:

> . . . The Prime Minister had resigned and flown off to Rome, his nerves frayed by the thankless task of guiding a newborn state. The king was ill, in seclusion; there was a rumor in the bazaars that he might abdicate. The whole government structure seemed about to collapse. I had just reached a vital point in negotiations for an air-base agreement. So when the Libyan cabinet asked me to fly to Italy and persuade the Prime Minister to return I cabled the Department urgently for permission to make the try.
>
> Time was of the essence, yet the hours ticked by without response. In Washington, the wheels ground methodically. Committee met with committee, weighing the pros and cons of my recommendation. The Pentagon had to be consulted. Policy factors had to be considered; so did tactics, in the light of progress to date on the air-base negotiations. Suggestions at a lower level had to be referred to a higher level for further discussion. I sent a second cable. No reply.
>
> Finally, I decided to act on my own. I boarded the plane of my Air Attaché, flew to Rome, and called on the Prime Minister at his hotel. With all the eloquence I could muster, I

urged him to come back and steer the ship of state through the storm, pointing out that the fate of his country — and our delicate negotiations — rested in his hands alone. He heard me in silence, still smarting from the political wounds which had caused him to resign. He would think it over; he would give me his answer that evening.

At eight o'clock I was again at the Prime Minister's door. His face was wreathed in smiles. He would do as I asked, and to mark the occasion he invited me to dine with him downstairs. With a load like lead off my mind, I was enjoying the repast when I spied an officer of our Rome embassy discreetly waving a piece of paper from behind the potted palms. I made my excuses, rose, and went over to receive the message — a priority cable to Tripoli, repeated to Rome for information. At long last, Washington had moved. There were my orders. *Under no circumstances* was I to follow the Prime Minister to Rome, for that, the Department feared, might be interpreted as interference in the domestic affairs of a sovereign country.

Earl E. T. Smith argues in *The Fourth Floor* that while he was ambassador to Cuba during the guerrilla activity of Castro the important issues that activity presented were not adequately presented to the Department's summit and never (as far as he knows) to the President or the National Security Council. Since he was trying to put together a group which would provide the Cubans with an alternative to Batista and Castro, it was important that this effort be adequately understood at the highest levels, either approved or rejected there, and if approved be given all possible support. Had Smith succeeded in Cuba, all necessity of a Bay of Pigs and a missile crisis with the Russians might have been avoided. Those on the front line can be stymied by the inadequacies of the pyramidal mass.

The lack of a basic plan handicaps every part of our establishment and no part more than the front line. If our overseas posts lack a master plan, as well as one for their particular country, by which to coordinate their moves with the Department, they are obviously going to work at a disadvantage, and they will be tempted to make only very cautious and timid moves. They will not want to be in the position of doing something that runs counter to what the Department or other posts may be doing. Until a basic plan is provided, the resources of our Foreign Service will not be more than marginally employed.

Consider our relations with Egypt in this connection. To be sure, not all the fault for poor relations is on our side, for Nasser plays a Machiavellian and often destructive game. But our own weakness is a factor. John S. Badeau, our ambassador to the UAR from 1961 to 1964, has observed that in less than a decade, beginning in 1952, the United States followed four different policies toward Egypt, the effect of which was to create the impression there that American diplomacy is unpredictable, not built upon clear principles, and indeed not built upon any consistent view of America's own interests. "The United States," says the ambassador, "must be more clear-sighted on defining for itself and the UAR what its vital interests are. A greater consistency of approach is needed. American foreign policy toward Egypt has been so erratic largely because Americans — like Egyptians — react rather than act. They do not recognize that it is possible for two countries to oppose each other on specific issues while maintaining a continuing and mutually profitable relation."

Conditions of service abroad are likewise an important ele-

ment of diplomatic success. Foreign Service officers are generally hard-worked. They have no time to study, to search for
long-term objectives and techniques. They have little time for
keeping abreast of what is happening outside the countries to
which they are posted. Yet, such are the far-flung interests
and responsibilities of the United States, that what our government does in one place is of great concern — sometimes
crucial concern — elsewhere.

I am aware that "overstaffed" posts may exist here and
there. But "overstaffed" in what sense? Consider the following observations of a career diplomatic officer, Ellis O. Briggs:

. . . Not long after the Communist seizure of Czechoslovakia, I was assigned to Prague as Ambassador. The State
Department asked me to survey the staffing needs of the Embassy "in the light of the changed situation" — meaning the
Communist coup d'etat of 1948, which had converted one of
the most friendly of European governments into one of the
most glowering and hostile.

Quickly ascertaining that in the Communist utopia the normal sources of diplomatic information are either cut off or
polluted, and that everything not published by the state is classified secret, there seemed to be little reason to maintain a
large staff in our Embassy in Prague. I recommended to
Washington that my inherited complement of eighty Americans be reduced, as a start, by one half. That is to say that the
roster be cut to forty, with the major part of the reduction to
be from agencies other than the State Department, since those
agencies were the ones supplying the soap-bubble blowers.

Pentagon personnel, for instance, accounted at that time for
thirty-three of my eighty colleagues. I suggested to Washington that henceforth ten soldiers ought to be sufficient to advise one Ambassador about military developments in Czecho-

slovakia. I also suggested that since Czechoslovakia was a landlocked country, lacking seacoast or navy, my Naval Attaché might just as well be assigned to Switzerland or Bolivia.

The State Department, after meditation, informed me that my recommendations were "interesting" and that there was "agreement in principle" that they ought to be implemented.

I was thus encouraged to embark on a campaign of the utmost frustration. The outraged squawks of my Prague colleagues quickly reverberated beside the Potomac, where every agency represented in my Embassy demanded of the State Department that the proposed reductions be borne by every other agency.

The State Department, which had instigated my investigation, and encouraged my recommendations, promptly went into a terrified tailspin. After six months, and an expenditure of effort on my part sufficient to have built, single-handed, a bridge across the Vitava River, I had managed to reduce my overblown staff by two persons — from eighty to seventy-eight.

At which point the Communists, ignorant of my hassle with Washington over personnel, and believing that they were doing the American government in general and the American Ambassador in particular the greatest possible disservice, suddenly declared five-sixths of the Embassy personnel *personae non gratae*. That is to say — unwelcome people. Czechoslovakia gave the Embassy two weeks in which to evacuate sixty-six of my seventy-eight colleagues, with their families, pets and belongings.

A *personae non gratae* declaration is one of the few things in foreign affairs that is not debatable, and the State Department had no choice but to comply. We got the sixty-sixth member of the staff across the border at Rozvadov within the prescribed time limit, and I sat back to enjoy the first unobstructed view from my Chancery since reaching Czechoslovakia the previous autumn.

They were a picked group, the twelve people selected from

seventy-eight. It was the most efficient mission, with the highest morale, of any in which I have been privileged to serve. Everything that was needful or important was accomplished with a minimum of friction and delay. No longer was it necessary to refer matters to a "country team" or to an interagency committee. We had the perfect response whenever a crackpot order was received from Washington: we "regretted that with our reduced staff it was unfortunately not possible" to investigate the rumor that the hop louse was lousing up the hop crop in the Sudetenland.

Moreover since the Czech Government now undertook to harass American citizens who were incautious enough to stray across the border, the State Department shortly declared the whole country out-of-bounds, and marked American passports to that effect. That meant that Embassy Prague was relieved of one of the most formidable burdens pressing today on diplomatic shoulders around the world: the weight of visiting firemen. (At my last post, in the off-election year of 1961, over two hundred members of the Senate and the House of Representatives visited the capital of the country where I was stationed, just between October and Christmas.) No longer did Embassy Prague have to drop everything to explain why the next-door neighbor of the Assistant Secretary of Health, Education and Welfare could not drive in a rented Opel with a West German chauffeur from Vienna to Warsaw via Brno, accompanied by his wife, three children and a brown poodle. In short, we had no visitors.

We ran, on the other hand, a taut and tidy operation, accomplishing what was needful to be done, keeping the State Department informed of what was going on, and even hazarding some guesses about what might happen in future. And we did all this with a smaller staff than I later found in many of the separate units and sections and subsections of the Embassies over which I presided after I left Czechoslovakia.

It may take a few more officials to take care of essential Embassy operations in a friendly country than it does in a Communist one, but the number needed — anywhere — is only a fraction of the number we have in over one hundred American diplomatic missions scattered over the globe. Today, almost everybody *is* playing diplomacy, and by permitting all these extraneous participants to invade the field, we have made it difficult to tell who has the ball, and even impossible at times to tell what team is defending what goal line.

The only American official who can rescue the conduct of our foreign affairs from the expensive confusion created by unneeded personnel abroad is the President himself, by directing the Secretary of State to take action.

This attitude raises many questions. Why, indeed, should the army and navy be so amply staffed in Prague? There are several answers. First, this is a part of the military's efforts to expose their officers to conditions abroad as extensively as possible. Second, in peacetime there *are* surplus military officers. The question is where the surplus should be quartered: in the United States, where their provincialisms can multiply ad infinitum, or abroad, where they can indeed be a bit of a nuisance but where they can observe things that military officers should know about these days? Does the fact that Czechoslovakia is a landlocked country *necessarily* mean that no one in the navy should be informed on the communist phenomenon as manifested in Czechoslovakia? Will not a naval officer so exposed be more informative and persuasive when called upon to advise his or another government? Or when he is among his colleagues of other navies? Does the career diplomat really believe the naval officer would be better spending his time behind a desk in Washington? Staffing requirements must be judged by the overall, long-ranged perspectives of the World Power we are and the responsibilities we must discharge.

As to overseas representatives of other departments and agencies of our government, the problem is not basically dissimilar, although superficially it may seem so. Since these departments and agencies are civilian, they need not operate for long periods with surplus staff. Nevertheless, their involvement in foreign affairs is real and their need, in Washington, is acute for personnel which has lived abroad, knows overseas conditions, has acquired something of a sixth sense of dealing with foreigners and — perhaps above all — has caught a glimpse of the diplomatic world into which they must fit their resources. If, indeed, their representatives abroad are "soap-bubble blowers," what better way is there to train them to become useful than actual service abroad? And what greater responsibility does an ambassador — or any other diplomatic officer — have than to contribute to that training?

The ambassador quoted does not state he was overstaffed with Foreign Service officers, but this is sometimes alleged by old-timers to be the case. I have never been in an overstaffed post, myself, or even in an overstaffed section of a post. I have always been in an overworked post, far too busy to keep up with the broader issues, accomplishments and failures of United States foreign policies and diplomacy and to take full advantage of the opportunities of leadership which came its way.

I am not making a plea for overstaffing our "front line." I am making a plea for staffing in the light of our responsibilities as a World Power waging a highly competitive struggle for the minds of men. One has to keep in view what the nation is trying to accomplish in this world — and what it must do in this matter of personnel if it is to lead and survive.

The career diplomat, it has always seemed to me, generally

needs considerably more imagination than he has about this subject. If he finds himself in a post overstaffed for the purpose of daily operations, he should be able to see that this provides just that fortunate bit of leisure in a tipsy-turvy world which can help him and his associates regain their perspective, extend their depth, refresh their whole approach to problems. It gives them time to do some real thinking, some serious reading, some basic analysis of our weaknesses and resources. Successful diplomacy is not simply a matter of efficient daily performance. It is not just a matter of "a taut and tidy operation" — not just a matter of what is "needful or important" for the week. It is what is needful for our nation over the long pull — the next five years, the next ten years at least. The communists understand this.

Whenever I am told that a post is "overstaffed" I always think of what Val Peterson did when President Eisenhower appointed him as our ambassador to Denmark. Finding his staff far from intellectually up-to-date he instituted a reading program. He had officers read and at staff meetings analyze books for the benefit of other officers. He stimulated discussions. Among other things, this led to a healthy atmosphere of dissent. It was an ingenious device for getting some of the attitudes of mind we desperately need in our diplomacy.

I doubt if Governor Peterson would want to be classified as an intellectual. He had had to work for his education in Nebraska and to rise to the governorship of his state. But he knew, as David Eugene Thompson knew, that you have to read and read hard to make yourself a leader in international affairs. It took him but a few days to sense that this concept was missing in his mission.

I have met but few career diplomatic officers who understood this. I have never heard of une who, as principal officer in his post, introduced a reading program. The Foreign Service Institute has never started one. Yet many an old-timer can be found to complain of a surplus staff which he doesn't know what to do with. He has opportunities of developing officers he does not so much as perceive. In this lies a source of our "no win" inadequacy. In such attitudes, preoccupation with the daily round, distaste for training, and tendency to nibble around the edge of problems instead of taking large bites, lie some of the reasons Presidents and Secretaries of State — and other departments — find their views inadequately presented abroad. Here lie some of the factors which account for those gaps between policies pronounced and policies executed which mystify foreigners and create doubts as to our ability to lead. The front line of the Department cannot but reflect the weakness of the Department itself.

CHAPTER 8

Of Gulliver in Lilliput

ONE OF ITS more serious problems, the State Department feels, is the President. He reciprocates this feeling heartily. The gulf between the two, which can be sizable and dangerous to the nation, has both political and psychological causes.

From the time a man declares his candidacy for the Presidency, one can see that a gulf exists between him and the diplomatic establishment. It continues to exist, ever widening, to the day he is inaugurated. He is rarely well-informed about the diplomatic establishment. Once nominated by his party, he is offered by the White House incumbent the briefing facilities of both State and CIA. But presidential candidates are wary of this. They prefer as complete freedom as possible in campaigning. Making points and making them stick for three or four months, whether they are right or wrong, is all too often regarded as the way to win the election. Moreover, such briefing as may occur during the campaign is on substantive issues, not on the organization, procedures or problems of the Department.

Once a candidate achieves the status of President-elect, he may still be wary. His contacts with the outgoing President are difficult if the two are of different parties, for the victor will be disinclined to blur the image he has created of the incumbent's inadequacies. Contacts with the State Department are often remote indeed, and at best they are limited to indirect contacts via the Secretary-designate of State or, if the President-elect is slow in selecting this associate, to a lower-echelon assistant and task forces who convey to him all too little insight into the strategies and needs of the diplomatic establishment.

The truth of the matter is that the President-elect prepares the initial elements of his program, decides his budget for the coming fiscal year, makes appointments to the State Department and ambassadorial posts — may even initiate foreign policy and diplomatic decisions — without making full use of the very organization that is specifically charged with advising him on foreign affairs. He comes to the Presidency and begins to wield its immense power almost as though the diplomats did not exist. What should be his right arm in foreign affairs is hardly more than an unfamiliar, dangling appendage. That this is extraordinary goes without saying. That it is inherently hazardous for the nation is obvious. The wonder is not that a Bay of Pigs fiasco occurs, but that it does not occur more often.

A certain lack of initiative on the part of the State Department is involved in this situation. The very Department which makes a point of knowing and cultivating influential leaders abroad makes no effective effort to do the same at home. It has found no way of establishing close contact with the one man who will most influence its future — and the nation's — so as to acquaint him, fully and directly, in advance of his assumption of responsibilities, with the strategic plans in force, tactics currently in operation, those envisaged for the immediate future, and the Department's own resources and needs. Thus the President, more often than not, comes to the White House sharing the popular attitude toward the diplomatic establishment, which amounts to uneasiness at best. History shows, indeed, that the more active and vigorous a leader he is, the more severe may be his lack of confidence in the Department. As we have seen, there is good reason for this feeling, but the Department, secure in its feeling of superior knowledge and abilities in foreign affairs, is unable to comprehend such skepticism and attributes it to ignorance. The chasm yawns.

A second factor arises from the President's nature. He is a politician. Departmental officers, on the other hand, are not. They have in fact considerably insulated themselves from politics.

The politician keeps one eye on the next election, which the Department ignores. The politician keeps tab on votes in Congress, not only on foreign issues but on the whole range of his program, while the Department assumes the high ground of what is best for the country. The politician is also sometimes involved in situations which make him appear to act the clown with redskin headgear or coonskin cap, while the other, too far from domestic politics to view such spectacles with understanding, only shudders to think how such tomfoolery will appear abroad.

Being a politician, the President comes to his office with commitments. Among these are debts of support payable in jobs. And there's the real rub, for top diplomatic positions are among the patronage prizes.

If we remember how concentrated is the ambition of the careerists for these, we can have no difficulty in visualizing the intensity of the conflict. The fact that diplomatic assignments are no longer soft and plush has only aggravated the career officers' feelings, for they are more aware of this change than the amateurs and all the more bitterly resent the imputation that these highest-echelon responsibilities demand little specialized knowledge. When the amateur's lack of preparation for his assignment extends so far as to make him appear ridiculous before the Senate Foreign Relations Committee and thus before the whole world — such as the president of a department store chain who could not so much as pronounce the name of the Prime Minister to whose country he would shortly be going — personal feelings are aggravated by a keen sensitivity about national dignity.

Within the diplomatic establishment a kind of scoreboard of appointments is kept with hawklike attentiveness: one political appointment, one career; two political appointments, three career. It has been known for a career officer who could not make the ambassadorial grade to circumvent the test of competence by quitting his career, contributing generously to a party — or perhaps to both parties — and emerge as a President's political choice for an ambassadorial post. This adds insult to injury and lowers the Department's estimate of White House judgment. If a President knows so little as to violate the Department's considered judgment on so demonstrable a matter as an individual's performance over the years, what *does* he know better in diplomatic appointments than the Department? That the Department's judgment is based upon efficiency reports not always as perceptive and equitable as they should be and subject to political influences of an internal variety does not occur to the denizens of Olympus.

What the diplomatic officers fail to keep in mind, in their relations with the President, is that diplomacy is just as much a personal matter with him as it is with them. He, like them, wants the "feel" of international problems, personalities, events. He wants more than memoranda; he wants personal relationships; he wants personal insights from men he knows. He therefore must have diplomatic representatives abroad who are not befriending a fraternity but primarily serving him. He does not want ambassadors whose allegiance is divided between an institution to which they are beholden for assignments or promotions, and the interest he considers to be uppermost; he wants only men attached to the latter. This is a hard thing to get across to career officers, and the Department is very obtuse about it. As in so many matters, it is so concentrated upon what it wants that it cannot place itself in the position of the President and think in terms of what *he* wants and needs.

Nor is the kind of diplomacy which Presidents need something that can be produced wholly by the State Department. It must consist of personal as well as institutional competence. It must be fed by individualists who can contribute fresh ideas. It must include not only a knowledge of foreign affairs and diplomacy but political sagacity and a sense of action, and personality. A President does not want conventional men with fraternal prejudices, so anxious to avoid offending colleagues that they cannot act with the decisiveness that great events demand. He must enlist talent that is as free as possible of narrow institutional or career interests.

The man whom the President appoints as Secretary of State is very important in this context. There have been follies in such appointments, but none in recent times. The emergence of foreign affairs as one of the primary concerns of the Executive emphasizes the importance of finding a man who shares his President's views, a man who has enough experience and intellectual drive to lead at least the top of State's unwieldy establishment and spread as many of the President's ideas throughout its lower echelons as possible.

But a problem arises at this very point. For a President seldom confides even to a trusted Secretary of State the choice of top-level Departmental associates. He himself appoints the Under Secretary of State, sometimes Deputy Under Secretaries and even Assistant Secretaries, all in the effort of distributing patronage and creating many pumping stations for his ideas. Some of these stations prove adequate for the President's immediate purposes, although they may not be so for basic Departmental reform. Others fail to last. For want of adequate knowledge and adeptness some falter and must be replaced. Such failures augment the Department's doubts about the President's grasp of people and foreign affairs. If the Secretary of State himself is not effective, or if he is a prima donna interested primarily in making a place for himself in history, these errors of appointment have an aggravated effect.

The role of the Secretary in bridging the gulf between his Department and the Executive Mansion can seldom be impressive. He generally knows too little of the Department for this. Even a "good" Secretary, as we have noted, is good only in some respects: he is faulty or even poor in others. He is almost uniformly deficient in effective understanding and management of the Department. The most he can do generally is to spot the needs of the President and bear down hard enough on these to keep his White House relations satisfactory. If, as Dulles did, he makes it a daily practice to drop by the Executive Mansion for an end-of-the-day confabulation, he may succeed in creating a sufficiently favorable impression of himself to cause the deficiencies of his establishment to recede in importance. But no really knowing President is ever deceived by this, which is why Eisenhower created the Operations Coordinating Board.

Presidents have another technique for bridging the gulf. They can sick their personal assistants onto the Department. These include not only an adviser on national security affairs, who may take a leading role in critical international situations, but other assistants who may prompt and pressure the diplomats on a wide variety of things. This can reach anarchic proportions.

The basic development in the Presidency effected by the avalanche of social problems in the 1930s was a transformation of that office from essentially a one-man operation into an institution. The heavy burdens of the President gave rise to a sizable White House staff and eventually, in the late 1930s, a whole Executive Office. This came to include not only an enlarged White House staff and the earlier established Bureau of the Budget but a Council of Economic Advisers (created in 1946), the National Security Council (1947), the Operations Coordinating Board (during the Eisenhower Administration), and other agencies which float in and out of the Office as times and problems change. It is today an impressive officialdom of over one thousand persons.

Such an Office places in the President's hands a ready instrument for projecting his ideas into virtually every level of the government. The White House staff, even the President himself in the Kennedy Administration, was known to telephone inquiries and suggestions as far down in State as to desk officers. The President's ability to thrust at the smugness of State and its defensive walls has thus been increased, and it is now limited only by the size and experience of the White House staff, the number of working hours a day, and the number of problems which rise to the White House level or which the staff can pull up to that level.

If this makes the President feel a little easier, it does not the State Department. Far from it. A White House staff can magnify both confusion and negative attitudes within the Department. In part, this reaction reflects State's inadequacies — a failure to think along with the President, to place itself in his position and consider what *he* needs rather than what he owes it as the permanent staff of experts in foreign affairs. It also reflects its failure to plan and adequately staff out its tactics. But in part, it reflects the lack of familiarity in the White House with foreign affairs. In any case, State is often irritated and bewildered, rather than invigorated, by the jabbing and probing of the President's staff, finding it a meddling intrusion instead of a stimulating exercise of coordination and leadership.

The confusion is amplified by a doubt in the minds of Departmental officers as to how far a communication from some part of the Executive Office represents a Presidential order or even a serious Presidential interest. Since White House staffers are engaged in a more or less active competition with one another for the President's favor, each is tempted to over-quote the President so as to get a desired result which can be a feather in his cap. He can make up a Presidential instruction or overshade a real one. This situation is aggravated when a President takes a Machiavellian pleasure in playing off people against one another, including their own staffers, as was true of Franklin D. Roosevelt.

Dean Acheson has given an example of the confusion that can thus arise:

> . . . On one occasion a note from a member of the White House staff informed me that the President had learned that a certain foreign service officer was stationed in an African "hardship post" and wished him transferred to a more healthy spot. I took the note to my next meeting with the President. Before showing it to him, I said that I wanted to know whether he had, indeed, issued this instruction, in which case it would, of course, be obeyed. In doing so, I pointed out, other changes of personnel would become necessary and it might be desirable to refer the whole series of decisions to the White House, although they hardly seemed worthy of the President's time. He read the note, tore it up, and we went on to the next item.

This kind of direct checking with the President is not always available to the head of the Department and never to his subordinates on the lower floors. Furthermore, Mr. Acheson's example was related to a relatively simple question. Confusion can be created on larger, more complicated issues, with disastrous consequences not only in the State Department but in our overseas service and in our relations with other governments. Nothing in our whole Government can call in question more sharply our capacity for consistent, intelligent leadership than the self-assured but chaotic moves of the President's staff.

De Lesseps S. Morrison, the politically sophisticated mayor of New Orleans who became, under President Kennedy, U. S. Ambassador to the Organization of American States, provides an illustration of this. He accuses a White House staffer, Richard Goodwin, of naïveté in falling for a Cuban ploy at the Punta del Este conference of 1961. The ploy brought about a secret meeting between Goodwin and the communist theorist Ernesto "Che" Guevara, even though such a meeting apparently had been expressly forbidden to the American delegation in its instructions from the President and Secretary of State. Weirdly enough, the "secret" meeting was attended by high-ranking Argentine and Brazilian diplomats and by two Brazilian journalists.

Morrison says Goodwin was noncommittal at the meeting, but the damage was done when Argentine President Frondizi subsequently held a secret meeting with Guevara on the same subject, coexistence. When the Frondizi meeting leaked to the press, the Argentine military, anti-Castro to the core, exploded in rage. Frondizi then went on national television to reiterate his pro-Westernness and justified his discussion with Guevara on the grounds that a U.S. representative had met with him, too. The whole impression given to Latin Americans was that the United States furtively considered accommodation with Castro feasible or at least worth exploring while taking publicly the opposite position in the Conference. Morrison adds that the results "were to plague us for months and almost cause us to fail in what I consider a major achievement of the Kennedy Administration, the ousting of Cuba by the OAS from inter-American society."

The inadequacies of the relationship between the President and State are reflected in periodic expansions of the White

House staff. Whenever there appears lack of competence in a crucial area, the vacuum is filled by the Chief Executive. Thus, in 1951, military and disarmament matters forced the President to add to his staff an Office of Mutual Security, headed by Averell Harriman. Following the abolition of the Operations Coordinating Board, the President's staff had to assume more and more of the chore of striving for greater integration of policies and coordination of efforts in foreign affairs.

President Kennedy saw in the Alliance for Progress, which had been conceived by the Eisenhower Administration, one of the more promising advances in foreign affairs. Accordingly, he had his staff push on it. Unfortunately, the willingness of his staffers exceeded their experience and maturity. The harder they pushed, the greater the confusion they generated. Lines of responsibility became so fuzzed up that desk officers and office directors in State did not know which way to look for orders, to their own superiors or White House staffers.

Unable to cope with the increasing anarchy, the Assistant Secretary in charge of Inter-American affairs, a career diplomatic officer, was shored up by the assignment to his bureau of one of the White House assistants, who was to work as deputy. The deputy was ambitious, enjoyed the prestige of White House identification and kept a communication line with the President's mansion, as well as with ambassadors to Latin American countries whose acquaintanceship he had made while in the Executive Office. The confusion increased. The unlucky Assistant Secretary was hoisted abroad as an ambassador, his humiliation, of course, diminishing his stature and influence in his new position. This did not help the President's diplomacy, a fact of which the White House staffers seemed oblivious.

The successor of the hoisted diplomat was not his deputy, he being, by common admission, too little experienced for the job. A competent, hard-nosed civil servant in the Department was made Assistant Secretary, but he stipulated, as a condition of his acceptance of the post, that his deputy's White House line be transferred to him and all communications with ambassadors go through his office. This restored order. It also terminated the glamour of the deputy's assignment which was soon changed to fragments of other tasks until he eventually returned to the White House. However, a single misstep of the new Assistant Secretary put him into Presidential disfavor and he, too, was hoisted abroad. Whether the misstep was only a pretext seized upon by White House intrigue is not known and the very uncertainty adversely affected the Department's morale and relations with the President.

The relations between the dynamic, pushing Kennedy staff and the Department became so trying that the young President made the unprecedented move of appearing before a meeting of the Foreign Service officers in an attempt to clarify his position. He reminded the officers that the Constitution conferred upon the President, not upon the State Department, the direction of the nation's foreign affairs and took pains to quote the original legislative enactment setting up the Department, thus adding Congressional and historical corroboration to his point. He quoted his grandfather's axiom that those who could not stand the heat of the kitchen had better get out — and over two hundred experienced diplomats shortly did. It was an altogether painful episode and one which neither added to America's diplomatic luster nor went to the real point of vexation. The problem was not Constitutional or statutory nor even ability to stand the heat of the President's kitchen. The problem was how to manage our foreign affairs sensibly and intelligently, in orderly fashion, so as to instill in our career officers the highest degree of initiative, vigor and effectiveness abroad without sacrificing consistent planning. That problem is no more to be solved by the Constitution or statute than by general axioms.

Similarly, another technique of the President in bridging the gulf between himself and the Department has helped the Chief Executive but startled and confused the diplomatic establishment, not to say foreign governments. This is by the use of personal, unofficial advisers and emissaries. Wilson had his Colonel House to travel abroad, listen, talk and bring back personal impressions. The diplomatic fraternity called him Colonel Mouse. Franklin D. Roosevelt had myriad operators of this kind. He also converted ambassadors to personal informers who either presumed or were instructed to bypass the State Department, thereby starving it of essential information and further exacerbating relationships. By using Harry Hopkins (who also had a profound instinct for, and mastery of, national politics) he initiated foreign studies and negotiations which the diplomatic establishment never knew existed. This was carried to such a point that at the very beginning of a crucial war in which our full diplomatic and military resources were needed, the White House operator in important matters virtually suspended the diplomatic establishment.

This Presidential bypassing of the diplomatic establishment is not a recent phenomenon, although the State Department tends to regard it as such, and is therefore distracted by recent experience from examining it as a basic, long-standing problem. If one goes back to the beginning of this century, one finds Theodore Roosevelt operating with considerable independence. This is not so far back in our history as to raise doubt about the current relevance of the problem, nor so recent as to create any illusions about how long this problem has existed.

When Roosevelt decided to intervene in the Russo-Japanese war to preserve an equilibrium of forces in the Far East, he made the decision and conducted the negotiations himself, completely circumventing the State Department. He replaced the American ambassador to Russia by a close personal friend whose astuteness he trusted, and in Washington he dealt directly with the friendly Japanese ambassador, as well as the influential Baron Kentaro Keneko, a Harvard classmate. On his own he endeavored to enlist the collaboration of the British and German governments and when he failed in this he engaged the help of personal friends in the foreign diplomatic corps in Washington. He dispatched his Secretary of War, not his Secretary of State or anyone from the diplomatic staff, on a mission to Japan to reinforce in Tokyo the persuasiveness of his efforts. When, by these various means, he got the peace conference he wanted, at Portsmouth, New Hampshire, he continued to make his good offices available, successfully climaxing a masterful diplomatic maneuver with a settlement of the war.

In the midst of this, Roosevelt detected symptoms of a similar problem in Europe. With France's ally, Russia, involved in war, Germany decided to challenge Gallic hegemony in

Morocco. Tension mounted and the President feared the German army might again attack France, not only jeopardizing his negotiations in the Far East but thrusting Germany forward to European domination, thereby upsetting both the European and the North Atlantic balance of power. When Berlin, astutely prompted, asked him to intervene, Roosevelt agreed to help.

The President's correspondence and discussions with the German and French governments in this affair were kept secret from all but a very few trusted friends, among whom the Secretary of State was not included. Nor were our ambassadors to France and Germany included. Personal diplomacy was this and secret as well — secret even as to the President's own government. It was hardly healthy but Roosevelt succeeded in bringing about the Algeciras Conference in 1906. Moreover, he planned the Conference's agenda, sent American diplomats to participate, offered to mediate at a critical juncture and rescued the Conference from a serious deadlock.

This, again, led to a brilliant result, the deferment of a major European war for almost a decade. But it was not a diplomacy for which our career diplomatic establishment could claim credit. It was a diplomacy which in fact humiliated that establishment and should have flashed to it signals of urgent warning.

This was only a part of the warning, however. Domestic affairs, now more intertwined with foreign, added to the diplomatic responsibilities of the President, and Roosevelt demonstrated how a President's resourcefulness in domestic matters had to equal his diplomatic skill, if friendly relations with foreign nations were to be preserved. In 1906, the year of the

Algeciras Conference and a year after Portsmouth, the San Francisco school board decreed the segregation of Japanese children in public school. The Japanese people were infuriated, their emotions all the more aroused because of the President's earlier pressures upon their government to accept his international goals. The two countries' relations, already strained, approached the breaking point.

Barred by the Constitution from intervening directly in California, the President expressed in his annual message to Congress objections to the ordinance of the San Francisco school board. His remarks were so pointed as to evoke vehement reaction from Californians. Denunciation of the President rose to uproarious pitch, the *San Francisco Chronicle*, among the more vehement critics, characterizing him as "an unpatriotic President who united with aliens to break down the civilization of his own countrymen."

Undismayed, Roosevelt took up the gauntlet. He pressed his case with both vigor and skill. A Cabinet member — again not the Secretary of State — was dispatched to San Francisco to assist in reasoning with the local authorities. He bombarded the governor and legislators with messages of admonition. When he felt that he had been sufficiently persuasive, he invited the mayor and school board to Washington. There the pressure or reasoning — depending on the participants' point of view — continued until the logjam broke. The ordinance was repealed.

Fully aware that this did not reach the source of the trouble, Roosevelt turned again to external diplomacy. He intimated to the Japanese Government how helpful it would be to take the self-abnegating step of limiting the emigration of Japanese nationals to the United States. This was quietly negotiated, eventually to be embodied in notes effecting what came to be known as "the Gentlemen's Agreement."

This still was not the end of the domestic-foreign cycle. To show the United States was being understanding and not timorous, Roosevelt decided that the anger of the Japanese, however justified, needed to be cooled by means of a display of power. He let it be known that our battleship fleet would circumnavigate the globe and include Yokohama on its itinerary. Vociferous protest from a sector of American opinion which felt the move might sour rather than sweeten the situation, did not deter him and he was on hand to review the fleet as it steamed forth on its odyssey. Roosevelt later boasted: "Every particle of trouble with the Japanese government and the Japanese press stopped like magic as soon as they found that our fleet had actually sailed and was obviously in good trim."

Here was *realpolitik*. Here, also, was a clear demonstration of how many areas were involved in the formulation and execution of diplomacy — including cultural affairs of a local character. Something in all this should have tipped off the Department as to what kind of learning, experience and skills it should begin demanding of its officers and to get to work training its people accordingly. But the Department took no heed. It ambled along, allowing the gap between it and the Presidency — and modern diplomacy — to widen.

The gap remains a most serious one. The Department is tempted to think of the President simply in terms of its own needs. But his is a complex position. He is not only Chief of State and the most important of the nation's diplomatic officers; he is also commander of the armed forces and chief administrator of the nation. And as impressive as these Constitutional roles are, historical developments have added still others of an extra-Constitutional sort. He is spokesman of the nation and indeed its clearest single voice on a variety of matters. He has become party leader, as well as the principal architect of legislation, the preserver of the nation's peace at home as abroad, and to no small degree a manager of the nation's economy. It is difficult for the imagination to take all this in, and unfortunately the State Department's has been quite unequal to it.

All these roles must be played together, in harmony. What a President does in one role has repercussions in others. He must integrate all into one. He cannot be party leader at breakfast, legislative leader in mid-morning, chief of state in late morning, diplomat at lunch, commander in chief before his nap and chief executive after, manager of the nation's economy when the stock market has closed and only in the evening a kind of surveyor and summarizer of his total activities of the day. He must in fact be all things at all times to all people.

A nuance of this, as Professor Rossiter has pointed out, is that any one of the President's functions or roles "feeds upon and into all the others. He is a more exalted Chief of State because he is also Voice of the People, a more forceful Chief Diplomat because he commands the armed forces personally, a more effective Chief Legislator because the political system forces him to be Chief of Party, a more artful Manager of Prosperity because he is Chief Executive." At the same time, as this scholar has observed, these various powers or roles compete with one another and inadequate synthesis can cause considerable difficulty. "The roles of Voice of the People and Chief of Party cannot both be played with equal fervor, as Mr. Truman proved on several occasions" — and as Woodrow Wilson demonstrated in the election of 1918 — "while to act as Chief Diplomat but to think as Chief of Party, as Mr. Truman did in the Palestine crisis of 1948, can throw our foreign relations into indelicate confusion."

Although leader of his party, the President must maintain in foreign affairs a high degree of bipartisanship. The State Department must assist him in this. But to do so it obviously can no longer take refuge in any generality that "foreign affairs have to be kept out of politics," to quote Cordell Hull, nor can it continue the conventional attitude that its officers require no special training with respect to the Presidency and its needs. The President should not have to turn elsewhere — all too often to the military establishment — for the performance of responsibilities which the diplomats should themselves be trained to assume. He should not have to turn to his Secretary of War rather than his Secretary of State to reinforce his negotiating efforts in San Francisco or in Tokyo, or to his Secretary of Defense and military officers for missions and judgments with respect to Vietnam which are political in nature or largely so, or to a general for proposals of how State can best solve its coordinating role in the Federal community.

Those who rise to the Presidency do so through a political process, one of decision, maneuver and action. Presidents are disposed to project this process into diplomacy. Because the Department has lagged so obviously, they have sought extra-Departmental assistance. But diplomacy is more than politics. It is politics practiced in a foreign environment, conducted with peoples whose psychological makeup differs from our own, peoples who are enmeshed in different cultures, and even in different time-spans.

In dealing with foreigners, therefore, a President can be a fish out of water. He needs the most subtle prompting and must display the most sensitive receptivity to prompting. Even if he has lived through some international adventure, as Franklin Roosevelt lived through the occupation of Veracruz by American forces when he was Assistant Secretary of the Navy, the depth and persistence of local feelings can escape him, as they did Roosevelt when, years later, he appointed as ambassador the man credited with that deeply resented occupation. These are the things on which a President needs advice and guidance. On his part, he must never assume he is as familiar with foreign politics as with domestic. As to the former, his guiding motto must be: "Stop, look and listen to the State Department."

But the State Department must put itself in a position to advise and act — not by clichés, not by mere improvisations, not simply by hunches (although hunches are important) — but by political sentience, by historical knowledge, by specialized experience, all having continuity and all being related to large, strategic plans. The President's responsibilities demand that he be a thoroughly realistic man. He cannot be adequately served by conventional attitudes, by operating procedures which deny continuity of knowledge, deep insights, adequate follow-through and anticipation of crises. He cannot be served by decisions which, because routine-minded, disregard and frustrate his own decisions.

A simple yet illuminating example of the problem State presents to a President every day of the year arose during the mounting crisis in Vietnam. The President decided early in 1964 that our personnel needs in that country were to have priority over all others. An officer doing some of the most important work in our embassy in Saigon came to the end of his two-year tour of duty a few months later and, in searching for his replacement, the Department dutifully assigned one of its most outstanding officers in that particular line. There the Department's imaginative follow-through ended.

The officer assigned to Saigon was in Africa. He had never served in Vietnam or even in the Far East, had had no dealings with those areas in any capacity and was as uninformed of them as one could be. He should have been promptly released from his African post so as to be meticulously prepared in Washington for his new and critical responsibilities. Instead, he was held at his post because the man who was to replace him was claimed to be needed in Brussels, where he was an assistant to another officer — not a key officer, note, but simply an assistant to an officer. His duties were not in fact pressing but personal strings were pulled by his superior to retain him longer.

This delayed the departure from his own post of the officer destined for Saigon and when he finally got to Washington en route to Vietnam he had insufficient time to take either the counter-insurgency course or the special course on Vietnam offered by the Foreign Service Institute. He could still have prepared himself, albeit inadequately, by taking a part of these courses but he found himself detailed to serve in the Bureau of African Affairs to replace an officer permitted to leave for his next post. The result was, the officer destined for Saigon in the midst of our hard, developing crisis there, arrived at his post with virtually no preparation by the State Department for his complex duties. The Department did not even brief him save in a most casual way. He learned a little about Vietnam by seeking out the friend of a friend in the Defense establishment who had recently returned from Vietnam. In the meantime, the officer he was to replace in Saigon had already left, to serve on nothing more critical than promotion boards in the Department, thereby suspending the important work which he had been doing in Vietnam and which his successor was intended to continue. This appalling record would be bad enough if the President had not laid down a policy declaring our needs in Vietnam to have priority over all others. In the face of that policy, the record suggests how Presidential policies are frustrated by routine minds in State's pyramidal mass. The Gulliver of the White House is all too frequently defeated by the strings of the Lilliputians.

CHAPTER 9

Different Worlds

CONGRESS and the State Department inhabit different worlds, a phenomenon derived not only from their form as established by the Constitution and from their function, but from political and psychological factors as well.

Constitutionally, Congress operates in a legislative world, State in an executive. This division induces an unfortunate separatist spirit which flares up now and again in the form of jurisdictional jealousies. These jealousies substitute rivalry for the team play badly needed in foreign affairs. Worse still is the Congressional suspicion of State which this division generates. There is always a feeling on Capitol Hill that the Executive branch is withholding something from the legislative body that properly belongs to it, and when Executive reticence which must necessarily cloak some of our international negotiations is abused, as Congressmen feel it was at Yalta, suspicion turns to rage, making the separation of worlds far more than merely jurisdictional.

Politically and psychologically, the world of Congress is primarily that of the nation, or rather of its innumerable local and ethnic communities, with all their differing degrees of awareness of foreign affairs, their special interests, their prejudices and provincialisms. We should not push this point too far, for Congressmen have evolved (or have had brought to them by events) techniques of international exposure and activity; but in no small measure each Congressman must live with a locality. That locality is familiar from birth, inbred and instinctive, and of course decisive as to the Congressman's future.

The world of the State Department, on the other hand, is as far from local as one could imagine. It is global, not familiar from birth but, to no small degree, intellectually acquired. Since it is in great measure understood through an exertion of the mind, strong intellectual criteria are subtly injected into the Department's judgment not only of foreign affairs but of Congress itself.

Congress, moreover, moves in a world largely of have, favored of Providence, of the here and now. The Department inhabits a world for the most part of disinherited and rebellious peoples, whose social and psychological patterns are intricate and contradictory, and whose civilizations stand at widely separated points of evolution. A more difficult world would be hard to imagine.

If one puts these various factors together, he finds that Congress works in a world legislatively limited, relatively calculable and controllable, the State Department in an unmanageable no-man's world where over one hundred national executives and legislatures seek, amid great disorder and cross-purposes — including every war in which we have been involved since 1914 — to edge forward their respective claims of sovereignty and interest.

Such differences in worlds produce differences of primary

interest. One of the first questions a Congressman always asks is: how do you explain a given problem or policy to the people back home? How do you get their votes? A State Department officer demands: what is it in our national interest to do and what will other people accept, regardless of what Americans think and how they vote? Congressmen take a strong "America first" attitude, and while the State Department does not place America second, it seeks "America first" in international situations in which America cannot always emerge first. From such differences stem differences in judgment. What the Department may feel is a sensible agreement or position, Congressmen may not. Communication becomes difficult. "It is often easier," an Assistant Secretary of State for Congressional Relations has remarked, "to communicate U. S. intentions to a tribal chief in central Africa through a Swahili interpreter, or to Kuala Lumpur across 10,000 miles of cable and radio, or to the U. N. General Assembly with its diverse dialects, than across the two miles from Foggy Bottom to the Capitol."

An intriguing sidelight to this phenomenon is that State Department men and Congressmen have, strangely enough, marked similarities of temperament and working habits. Both operate in hand-to-mouth fashion, with minimal planning and internal coordination. Both are so hard-pressed by daily business that they have tragically little time for study and reflection. Each group of men is deeply responsive to fraternal sensibilities and indulges its members' foibles. Furthermore, both Congressmen and diplomatic officers are preoccupied with their own individual performance. Individual advancement, individual success mesmerize them. If the House of Representatives does not carry this so far as to be called "an assembly of melodramatic actors," as some observers have called the Senate, both houses nevertheless do have, as has the diplomatic establishment, such great interest in personal assignments, recognition, and deference, that Congress and State seem at times stages for prima donnas.

Both Congress and State, moreover, are wedded to time-honored attitudes and practices. Their operating procedures are so steeped in precedent that effecting change is difficult. This in turn affects their attitudes. Each feels that in its own establishment the going way is the eminently good way. Each tinkers with its habits and adjusts them in minor respects but for want of time and inclination to intellectual analysis each views any critic from within as a scarcely bearable heretic and any critic from without as a bumbling ignoramus.

Ironically, both establishments tend to be slack in supervising their colleagues' use of public funds. Each overlooks the beam in its own eye while all too ready to see the mote in the other's. Finally, neither can be said to enjoy considerable public understanding and confidence. Both suffer from the vicissitudes of an uphill struggle to command the nation's respect.

These are not insignificant similarities, but one would be naïve to think that the two organizations could be drawn together by them. The opposite is the case. The fact that Congress, facing reelection every few years, must work quickly and seek short-term results is no reason, in its opinion, for an executive department to do so. The diplomatic officers, having permanent tenure, are considered remiss because they do not take the long view and plan ahead. One of the reasons that officers were given career security in 1924 was the hope that the quality of their performance could be improved by removing the limitations of political vicissitude. Since the diplomats have continued to concentrate on the day's business, Congress has naturally felt a keen sense of disappointment.

Congressmen feel that their own tendency to emphasize personal and fraternal considerations is a product of their insecure calling. The removal of the diplomatic officers from politics was intended to abate, if not eliminate, politicking for assignments and promotions. The fact that this has not happened, and that Congress has had to intervene from time to time to reinforce the merit system in the diplomatic establishment, are particularly sore points on Capitol Hill.

Congress feels the same resentment about the failure of the diplomats to do the difficult work of research, study, and reflection demanded by foreign affairs. This failure has been inexcusably compounded, in the eyes of Congressmen, by the diplomatic officers' tendency to ignore such instruments as the State Department's own Bureau of Intelligence and Research expressly provided as a corrective to the situation. Congress sees the State Department as an organization which trots along the same risky path as itself, dealing with the future one day at a time, but without any of the excuses for doing so that the legislature has.

Apart from the failure of similarities to bring the two bodies together are divisive factors implicit in the different worlds in which they operate. Typical of these is the

> . . . great uncertainty about State on Capitol Hill; the average Congressman is apt to look upon the fellows in State as "cookie pushers" or "ivory tower boys." One is almost convinced that some Congressmen are suspicious of State Depart-

ment officials because they are able to speak foreign languages — which makes them in a sense foreigners, and hence untrustworthy. Certainly there is something about the manner of the garden-party variety of diplomat that baffles and bothers the average M.C. These are creatures out of another world; certainly they are not "folks," not the kind of people he knows back home.

While this was written fifteen years ago and is now subject to some qualification, it is still true to some extent, for the attitude stems from the American's innate distrust of diplomacy.

An ironic twist to this hostility developed from the sponsorship by Congressmen of a number of moral deviates for diplomatic and consular appointments before 1924 — before the commissioning of such overseas officers was legislatively required to be placed on a merit basis. There were, in other words, Congressmen who contributed to the very decline in responsible conduct of our foreign relations which their higherminded colleagues rightly deplored, and also to the disrespect for Congressmen in general which pervaded the diplomatic establishment.

Since Congress is a highly political organism, and State is not, the two have nowhere near the same degree of political sensitivity and aptitude. As Congressmen come to their positions through a hard, often bruising process, and win their seats as a result of sustained, concentrated effort, they take a dim view of the relatively vague preparation demanded by State for diplomacy. They cannot but entertain doubts as to the State Department's seriousness of purpose and view skeptically the ability of its officers to deal with foreigners who are as seasoned and adept in political maneuver as Congressmen themselves.

Aggravating these misunderstandings is the strong interest in purely local affairs which most Congressmen bring to their duties, a bias constantly reinforced by the pressures of local interests and organizations and Congressmen's own efforts to keep in touch with their constituents. "Congress is motivated and stimulated and concerned primarily by reactions of its citizens, local pressures, local conditions," one of its long-term members has said. One of a Congressman's chief tasks, another has observed, is "how to vote in the national interest and get away with it."

Yet if there is one thing most candidates for the diplomatic service know little or nothing of, it is precisely the local environment in which Congressmen must struggle for survival. If they have any knowledge of it at all, it is only a smattering. They have very little idea as to what their Representatives' and Senators' backgrounds and problems are with respect to foreign affairs. In fact, it is an exceptional candidate for diplomatic service who knows the names of those who represent him in Congress. Thus, a diplomatic officer and his Congressmen begin their careers in different worlds, and their thoughts rarely coincide because they move further and further away from each other as their careers progress.

Since the goal of a Congressman's competitors back home is to belittle him, he is not wholly free from the temptation to blurt out some piece of extraordinary or alarming information likely to make the headlines, thereby reassuring constituents of his alertness and importance. To gain stature with important journalists he may even leak confidential information which can seriously embarrass the Department and cause minor crises in our foreign relations. This can be done in utter, cynical disregard of the national interest. It can be done, also, for other reasons, but this is hard for the unpolitical minds in State to appreciate. For the most sincere and patriotic reasons a legislator may wish to place a piece of information or an opinion before the American public — or simply before the President. It may be a suggestion which he has sought in vain to impress upon the Department. It may relate to a step or negotiation by the Department which he feels is so unwise and so against the national interest as to justify his extreme measure. A few years ago, when Senator Ellender vented his strong opinion that Africans were gaining their independence in advance of their capacity to govern, it did not disturb him that he was infuriating African leaders, that the doors of their countries were being closed to him, and that our diplomatic establishment was so upset that it immediately issued a press release disassociating itself from the Senator's remarks and made plans to dispatch a special emissary to visit and comfort the offended governments. The Senator felt that he had succeeded in communicating to the President, to State, and to the nation — in a way more forceful than private, discreet methods — his judgment that our government had long been over-encouraging independence movements in Africa and Asia, contributing to graver disorders and more calls for U.S. intervention than would have arisen under a more cautious policy.

The subjection of Congressmen to the ordeal of public scrutiny accustoms them to a world of noisy dispute that is wholly alien to the diplomats. Winning their seats in such a world, legislators naturally feel that vehement controversy is not so hazardous to the nation's welfare as the diplomats believe. For the discreet approaches, quiet inquiries, discussions of views *sotto voce*, to which the latter are conditioned by temperament and experience, Congressmen are inclined to over-compensate by outspoken and blunt remarks.

While Congressmen are increasingly aware of the shrinking size of the world and have become more prudent, each indiscretion is now more destructive than before. The number of occasions on which Congressmen openly oppose the Department may have diminished, but in international politics, as in warfare, a legislator now gets a bigger bang for his buck.

A State Department officer tends to stereotype Congressmen, as they do him. He tends to feel that all legislators disrupt diplomacy, as if they were wild daredevils on some worldwide communications trapeze. He handles them with caution, and his caution is heightened by competition for position and promotion in the diplomatic establishment. One embarrassment arising from confiding in a Congressman is one too many when one is in competition with officers who have spotless records. When one adds to all this a gnawing Congressional doubt as to State's competence — even the degree of its security consciousness and plain, ordinary efficiency — one can understand the degree of sensitivity in the relations of the two bodies. This is why a Department civil servant dissatisfied with his superiors' decisions with regard to the security clearance of a diplomatic officer and unable to obtain what he deems a forthright reconsideration of the clearance, leaks his doubt to a Congressional committee. He knows he can get an explosive reaction. If State then dismisses the civil servant, a blaze is ignited on "the Hill" which usually demands the successive interventions of the Secretary of State and the President himself, neither of whom is able to extinguish fully the embers of suspicion.

The intertwining of foreign with domestic affairs has increased the magnitude of this problem in recent years. Foreign policies and diplomacy are brought to a legislative focus in many more than the two Congressional committees assigned to deal with "foreign affairs." The committees on agriculture have been led by surplus agricultural production into a whole area of international diplomacy. Those dealing with commerce, tariffs, aeronautics and outer space have been similarly involved in "foreign relations." Congress's Joint Committee on Atomic Energy deals with matters to which our allies and rivals are extremely sensitive. So do the military affairs committees. The House Committee on Education and Labor is more sharply sensitive to moves in the International Labor Organization than the House Committee on Foreign Affairs; and the same sensitivity characterizes the other committees whose areas of domestic concern involve them with specialized international organizations.

Do the communists promote anti-American riots in Bogota, Caracas, La Paz, Tokyo? Is there a communist threat to the United States in the Caribbean? Then a Senate committee investigates and reports. What committee? Foreign Relations? Military Affairs? No, not at all. The Judiciary Committee. Why the Judiciary Committee? It has a "sub-committee to investigate the administration of the internal security act and other internal security laws" of the nation and has reached out to matters of external security. Just as there is hardly a department or agency of the Executive Branch which is not involved in foreign affairs, so there is hardly a Congressional committee which is not.

For good measure, there is even a Senate committee on government operations, which is concerned with the operating problems and deficiencies of the Executive Branch, and has got deeply into the latter's handling of foreign relations. The result has been a series of hearings and studies of State and the Foreign Service more penetrating than any undertaken by the Senate's committee on Foreign Relations, or indeed by any other committee, Congressional or Presidential, since the Hoover Commission of twenty years ago.

Since each house has, in effect, a great many committees on "foreign affairs," some fairly sophisticated probing and spotting of weaknesses in our foreign policies and diplomacy occurs on Capitol Hill. When Secretary Rusk told the American Legion that "at least a half a dozen committees and subcommittees of Congress are looking us over all the time and in great detail" he was not drawing too long a bow. In fact, he was not drawing his bow long enough. There are considerably more than half a dozen, and they are manned by legislators with a far more sustained familiarity with their respective areas than any of the rotating State Department officers.

The charters and programs of the international organizations to which we belong aggravate this complexity. When the World Health Organization defines "health" as "a state of complete physical, mental and social well-being and not merely the absence of disease," its efforts obviously overlap with other international organizations likewise concerned with "social well-being," such as the International Labor Organization, the Food and Agricultural Organization, the United Nations Educational, Scientific and Cultural Organization, the World Bank, and the International Monetary Fund. This intertwining of interests and jurisdictions presents a real problem to the intelligent transaction of foreign relations, but it does not, in Congress's view, relieve the State Department from doing a first-class job of orderly management.

Congressional-State relations are further complicated by the fact that other Executive departments and agencies have strong ties with Congressional committees. The Agriculture Department obviously has need of such ties with the committees dealing with agricultural affairs; Commerce, with commercial affairs; Labor with labor, and so on. But the competitive, sometimes wayward interests of these Executive departments in foreign affairs may produce tugs-of-war on Capitol Hill that are more energetic than edifying, more helter-skelter than helpful. The Congressional committees, in turn, provide not only the Executive agencies, but lobbying and pressure groups as well, with focal points for pressing their claims. Such claims often concern subjects of mixed domestic and foreign interest. Sugar is a notorious example.

Recent events have helped somewhat to reduce the gap between Congress and the State Department. The convulsions of wars and depressions, obliterating much of the distinction between domestic and foreign affairs and thrusting large portions of our population overseas, have reduced the provincialism of Congressmen and their constituents and impressed upon the legislators the need for diplomacy and what it involves. The persistent threat to national survival and the dire requirement of international cooperation have eradicated suspicion of friendly foreigners and their cultures. Certain Congressmen have even become the principal generators of pressure upon the diplomatic establishment to perfect its knowledge of foreign languages, history, politics and civilizations.

Congress demands more and more time of the Secretary of State and his summit associates at committee hearings. More and more of their testimony is off the record and therefore more informative. Individual Congressmen have provided themselves with additional assistants having a background in foreign affairs and their committees contract with universities and foundations for studies in foreign affairs. The Legislative Reference Service in the Library of Congress has developed a large staff on foreign affairs, comparable to State's own bureau of research and, unlike State, Congress has no inhibitions about using it. The General Accounting Office is also available for overseas investigations.

Private organizations which study foreign affairs provide additional gap-filling facilities. They hold off-the-record, round-table discussions of American interests and policies with scholars, businessmen, White House staffers, Congressmen and representatives of State and other departments. An invited Congressman unable to attend may generally send a member of his staff or a member of an interested committee. These gatherings provide Congressmen with occasions to get a line on the thinking of State's lower echelons as well as to obtain a broad range of views from thoughtful segments of the public.

Nor let it be supposed that the legislators are ignored by the foreign embassies in Washington. Far from it. They are as fully members of the dinner and cocktail circuits as the diplomats. This is how the foreign representatives pick up their choicest insights into American politics and Congressmen some of theirs into foreign affairs. "In Washington," says a well-known and successful maker of the social rounds, "you can't separate business and pleasure. A word or two at a party can develop a mutual interest in a problem or a position. It is a vital instrument. It is the only place where the different segments of Washington life can be mixed."

In the course of the mixing, a Congressman may not only buttonhole foreign diplomatic officers; he can sometimes buttonhole the Secretary of State as well as lower-ranking officers of the Department. In turn, he can be buttonholed himself. Embassies do not socialize lightly. Nor do they limit themselves to direct approaches to Congressmen at their parties. They are in the business of "public relations" and their social gatherings are devices by which their local lobbyists can be introduced to the legislators of Capitol Hill.

The American public knows little of the competition given State by the indigenous representatives of foreign governments. Like the lobbyists for national interests, they are American citizens, sometimes lawyers, sometimes "public relations counselors," and their role is to provide information (or partial information), to call Congressmen's attention to obscure points of interest to their employers, to remind them of forgotten assurances given at a social gathering and even to offer political assistance, such as planting favorable stories in legislators' home-town newspapers. They are also on Congressmen's fund-raising lists and form the backbone of the growing business of Washington financing of political campaigns. The development of Congressmen's obligations to such people is one of the subtleties confronting the State Department's efforts to keep our foreign relations on an even keel.

As such lobbyists are American citizens, they can argue without being considered intruders and can intervene in legislation without appearing to be meddlesome outsiders. Their mistakes can be repudiated by their respective embassies without embarrassment. They are, in effect, local ambassadors, shadowy, elusive, but very real competitors with State and serious contributors to its burdens of coordinating our foreign policy decisions.

In this free-wheeling social life in Washington, Congressmen are generally more approachable than State Department officers, and they are eager to pick up the latest scuttlebutt. Moreover, they have a nose for politically significant leads, and they also know what to do with leads. They therefore find themselves getting clues, hints, information — and misinformation — from people who would not venture to share their latest buzz with the Olympian gods of State. As a consequence, a Congressman can sometimes be way ahead of State, as was the Senator who, in August 1962, first alerted the country to the existence of missiles in Cuba. State can pride itself on having more information at its disposal than any single individual — Congressman or otherwise — but it is not the amount of information that counts. It is the quality of the information and the quality of the political instinct that operates on it. What is done with information spells the difference between bureaucratic performance and quick, adept political action.

As valuable as are domestic connections with foreign affairs, Congressmen have overseas connections as well. They travel.

So do their staffs. So do their committee staffs. They penetrate to all but a few of the areas of the world, and they visit all but a few of our overseas posts. Exceptional is the trip which fails to yield a myriad of ideas on how our policies and diplomacy can be improved.

This migratory inquisitiveness can of course bewilder foreigners, whose parliamentarians enjoy no such privilege. But at the cost of some overseas incredulity, confusion and perhaps loss of respect, Congressmen get to be fairly well informed. They spot deficiencies and bring back to Washington a knowledge of our diplomatic establishment which sometimes exceeds that of the Secretary of State, who never gets around to more than a few of our principal posts and even then cannot inquire into their operations in detail.

This factor has also been responsible for some of the great surges of imaginative leadership in Washington. At a time when the Department was taking a narrow-minded attitude toward a staff inherited from the Office of War Information, Congress was sending to Europe a joint committee of eighteen members of the Senate and House to survey the overseas branch of that staff and its peacetime potential. The Smith-Mundt report which came from this trip and the conversion of Mundt, a Midwestern isolationist, to the vision of a broad informational and cultural program throughout the world, have been among the great postwar milestones of American foreign policy.

This worldwide Congressional foraging narrows in some ways, and widens in others, the division of Congress and State. To old-time career diplomats, such foraging smacks of a "proliferation of American officials abroad," to which they object.

It is too much of the phenomenon of "everybody playing diplomacy." There is also a question of numbers. Ambassador Briggs complains that over two hundred members of the Senate and the House of Representatives visited the capital of the country in which he was once stationed, just between one October and the ensuing Christmas.

Aggravating these conflicts is Congressional meanness in parceling out funds for the diplomats' own travel and representational needs. Funds for Congressmen's travel and indulgences en route never seem restricted. Nor does it seem ever to occur to them that their travel imposes upon posts the necessity of drawing upon their meager entertainment funds for the financing of the Congressmen's visits.

This presents a quandary our diplomats have never resolved. If they entertain Congressmen according to Congressionally-provided means, the visitors will judge it so niggardly as to be calculated offense. If they entertain Congressmen well, they will be deemed to be living off the high side of the hog. And whatever they do, Congressmen will jealously note they have domestic help, which few of them can provide their wives. "We don't want to pamper you people," a Congressman once said to me. Far from it, friend. You rub salt in our wounds.

In addition to costing our overseas posts money, Congressional visitors tax officers' already hard-pressed days and nights. Accommodations must be reserved for them, often in capitals of limited facilities. And woe to the officer who does not quarter a Congressman according to his expectations. In addition, Congressmen must be briefed, sometimes extensively, and transportation and escorts often provided. Posts have been known to be denied suitable conveyances by Congress but visiting Congressmen demand the best, and if travel in the hinterland of underdeveloped countries is desired, vehicles must be mobilized for that, too, and native inhabitants solicited for suitable accommodations.

If the urge to travel hit only committees that are obviously involved in foreign affairs, the numbers of Congressmen abroad would be more reasonable. But the urge comes over many members with only the vaguest link with our foreign policy. For instance, one might reasonably ask what a committee like the one on Post Office and Civil Service has to do with foreign affairs; but its chairman has come up with an answer. Federal employees work abroad, don't they? Does this not call for a study of "Federal personnel practices" abroad? Since any sensible study of "personnel practices" must be made with reference to substantive programs, even this committee gets into foreign policy and diplomacy and taxes our overseas posts accordingly.

Few indeed are committees and Congressmen unable to wangle trips abroad and it takes a lot of scandalous junketing to shock the diplomatic establishment and the American public. But shocks occur. A Congressman once headed for Europe purposedly to study equality of opportunity for Continental women. He began his researches at the elegant Crillon Hotel in Paris, moved to a fashionable seaside resort in Greece and, when criticism of his junket mounted in the United States, betook himself to Madrid where he announced his real purpose: to study the Common Market. Spain, of course was — and still is — outside the Common Market.

Extravagance goes so far as to include lame duck and retir-

ing Congressmen in this amiable pastime of squandering public funds. Between an election and the following session of
Congress these lost souls are comforted by the pleasures of
travel at government expense. "It is a practice which ought to
be stopped," more than one Congressman has protested, "for
by no stretch of the imagination is any legislative purpose ful-
filled." But committee chairmen have both fraternal considerations and precedents to hold them to the course of indul-
gence and they are not readily responsive to change.

When Congressmen and their staffers fail to hold their li-
quor like ladies and gentlemen, additional complications arise.
Their travel can stir up a hornet's nest of publicity adverse to
the United States and set back for a long time a post's efforts
to promote understanding and followship as well as the promotions of individual officers who may get entangled. Less
sweeping in effect but profoundly demoralizing to the diplomatic establishment is the less-than-ethical treatment of diplomatic officers by visiting Congressmen. I am thinking not
simply of the horrors of McCarthyism, which were not only
perpetrated in Washington but also carried abroad by the
Senator's staffers, who were all too faithful replicas of their
boss. I am thinking of the sneering Senator who completely
destroyed all respect for Congressmen among the junior officers of a post I once led. I am thinking of the Senator who,
having visited Korea as member of an inquiring subcommittee, took such violent objection to one of the briefing remarks
of our ambassador — a capable career officer — that his career
thenceforth became a prickly problem to himself and the Department. For years he could get no overseas assignment.
Good Congressmen, and good Congressional staffers, in their

travels abroad can do much good. Vicious ones can work havoc.

All these factors come to bitter focus in the appropriations process. State must have funds and these must come from Congressmen. First to examine State's annual appropriation requests on "the Hill " is a subcommittee of the House Appropriations Committee, whose chairman is John J. Rooney of Brooklyn. What Brooklyn thinks of diplomats is apparently very little and that little is vitriolic.

It must be said that the State Department is rarely well prepared for this recurring financial ordeal. Its propensity for rotation ensures that again and again its representatives are unable to answer subcommittee questions. "Much of this happened before I took over." "I am not familiar with the point." "This has been done (or not been done) for the two years I know of." Even in matters susceptible to clear, direct answers, the Department's representatives display a disconcerting tendency to hedge until a subcommittee member will say in desperation: "Why not say 'yes' or 'no'?" It may be that the subcommittee makes monkeys of State's representatives, but it is just as true that State permits it to do so. Its career officers rarely have the grasp of their business that Rooney and other long-term members of Congress have acquired. There is nothing that can give more comfort to our enemies than the transcripts of these deplorable hearings. And they occur once a year.

The Secretary of State leads off the testimony and is accorded a respectful attentiveness. Everyone recognizes he is doing the best he personally can. It is when the Deputy Under Secretary for Administration enters the scene, followed by Assistant Secretaries, Deputy Assistant Secretaries and office directors, that respect evaporates and gloves come off. Congressman Rooney has a sixth sense of the weaknesses of State, and this has been sharpened by his travels abroad. He cannot be fooled. This hard fact is something the diplomatic officers, in their unending rotations in and out of the Department, have never learned.

If there is one hard, thorough, politically perceptive study long overdue by State it is that of nationalism in Latin America, its bearing on American investments, on the Panama Canal and other strategic interests, and possible ways of countering its destructive impact. But witness what happened before the Rooney subcommittee when such a study was finally incorporated in the budget of the Bureau of Inter-American Affairs in 1964. The following exchange occurred:

> *Congressman Lipscomb.* Is this a usual practice of bureaus of the Department of State to contract for this kind of service?
> *Assistant Secretary of State Mann.* No, sir. We have not had nationalism of the kind we are talking about now in past years. It is growing every day.
> *Mr. Lipscomb.* This is a new arrangement where you start contracting for this type of information outside of the Department?
> *Mr. Mann.* Yes, this would be a contract, what we propose here, as against hiring consultants, which is the other technique. It is very hard for a man who spends 8 or 10 hours a day on his job to do the kind of work that should be done in this area.
> *Mr. Lipscomb.* Why would not this be a job for the Bureau of Intelligence and Research?
> *Mr. Mann.* Because . . . it calls for policy decisions and not just the accumulation of facts. I do not want to make a great

point out of this, Mr. Congressman. I derive nothing personal from this and if you think the studying of nationalism —

Congressman Rooney. It is not a matter of not concerning yourself with nationalism. How many people do you have in Latin America, about 1,700?

Mr. Mann. 767 Americans in the field.

Mr. Rooney. You have 1,500 people altogether between those in Washington and those in Latin America, and I would think one of their primary concerns would be nationalism. In addition, we have USIA, the Peace Corps, and I would expect all these people to be concerned about nationalism. So if we do not allow this $20,000 it does not mean you should not concern yourself with the subject of nationalism.

Mr. Mann. No, sir, I would not say that. The question is whether it is worthwhile to make a study in depth of what the problem is and the techniques that might be used in our own interests.

Mr. Rooney. We listened yesterday to the Bureau of Intelligence and Research and of [sic] some studies they had made in China. It so happened that I had dinner last night in a Chinese restaurant. A Chinese gentleman who had never gone beyond the second grade in high school in China — I do not know how old he is, perhaps about 50 — seemed to know as much if not more about Red China than what was contained in the studies we had before us yesterday.

Words could well fail the Department at this point, but it is the point to which it is reduced on virtually every appropriation request whether it is for serious research, a motor vehicle for a post or a shower curtain for an ambassador's primitive bathroom in Africa. It is the point which it can anticipate year after year and for which it can find no cure. Consequently, it finds itself with wholly inadequate funds to discharge its far-ranging, complex responsibilities. Not even obsolescent typewriters and computing machines can be replaced except after years of repeated request.

State complains that it receives from Congress less than one-half of one per cent of the $32 million spent by the United States Government for foreign policy research. This is indeed gravely disproportionate to State's needs. But what has State done to use the products of the 99.5 per cent of the $32 million not expended by itself? What initiative has it taken to lead the other agencies to a coordination of effort, so that the research of the other agencies is used as much as possible to fill the gap left by State? For years and years very little. Only in 1965 could it come to the Rooney subcommittee and report that it had — at the prodding of a Congressional committee — taken steps "to inject some coordination, advance planning, and discussion for the purpose of avoiding duplication, saving costs, minimizing waste, and promoting the most efficient possible use of overall Government resources in the field of research expenditures in foreign policy." In other words, it had finally set up a Foreign Area Research Coordination Group to get adequately acquainted with the research being done by twenty different Government agencies, make use of that research and thus bring to bear on its own needs these resources of the Government.

A basic element in this situation has been State's administrative and managerial performance. Congress has not been convinced of State's ability to manage itself efficiently and to make good use of such funds as are appropriated. Its members have uncovered too many instances in Washington and in posts around the world of slovenly practice, of commitments to mere routine, and of failure to analyze problems and needs.

Even to Congressmen favorably disposed toward the Department, it has appeared "loosely run." A Congressman like Rooney considers it "a fluid State." As a result, diplomacy has been not only denied funds, as no other sector of our national defense, but annually held up to ridicule in a public spectacle.

When Henry L. Stimson became Secretary of State in 1929, he found the morale of the diplomatic service badly shattered. Because of a lack of funds more than a third of the Foreign Service officers whose efficiency records entitled them to promotions had not been promoted for periods of up to six years. Discouragement and discontent were rife. The condition extended to the clerical staff of the Service where a formidable rate of resignation had set in, the losses including many of the most experienced and valuable people. In one of those rare instances of a Secretary putting his shoulder to the administrative-Congressional wheels, Stimson went to work on Congress and got the needed funds.

Then what happened under Stimson's successor?

As great a Secretary of State as Cordell Hull proved to be in many respects and as astute a Congressman as he had been, he let the State Department down in important respects. He took a wholly unrealistic position concerning the management and financing of the establishment. As to the one, he wanted no part of it. As to the other, he recorded his position as follows:

> Wilbur Carr, the Assistant Secretary in charge of our budget, continued the policy of economy in the Department and kept asking Congress for just enough when other departments were asking for more than enough. The Appropriations committee became accustomed to slicing down the estimates

of other departments and treated us the same way, unfortunately forgetting that we were requesting only what we really needed. In the face of greatly expanded demands for the State Department services here and abroad as world conditions descended toward chaos, the Department was to struggle along desperately with inadequate funds. The appropriations for our Department of Peace were less than 1 per cent of the appropriations for War and Navy.

"Unfortunately forgetting." Through the decades the diplomatic establishment has been victimized by unfortunate forgetting. Through the decades it has had to "struggle along desperately with inadequate funds'" perpetuating conditions of service intellectually crippling and certain of only one result: inadequate performance.

One must keep in mind that no matter how good are a President's and Secretary's relations with Congress these rarely inure to the benefit of the Department as a whole. Whatever confidence the legislative body has in these two officials does not alter its basic, continuing recognition of inadequacy in the pyramidal mass of the diplomatic establishment.

It is for this reason that Presidents find it inexpedient to intervene in the appropriations process. President-elect Kennedy took Mr. Rooney on a cruise in the hope of mellowing him in congenial Irish society, but Mr. Rooney was not about to mellow. He has his facts and those facts tell him that the Department is not doing its job in entirely too many respects. Until it does, it will get no generous treatment from the Representative of Brooklyn or his associates.

In the realm of foreign affairs as a whole State-Congressional relations are somewhat better than in the area of appropriations. Here, the President combines his efforts with those of the Department to keep Congress informed on substantive matters of policies and events. Sometimes with the President reinforcing the Department, sometimes with the President leading the way, considerable effort is expended to keep Congress abreast of the more critical international developments. Congressional leaders are invited to the White House for breakfast, for midmorning conferences, for evening get-togethers. The President briefs them, his staff briefs them, the Secretaries of State and Defense brief them. These sessions often assume the character of National Security Council discussions. President Johnson has in fact taken the step of inviting Congressional leaders to meetings of the Council. This carries Executive briefing very far indeed. All this helps to bridge the two worlds at times of crises and also to develop bipartisan support for the Executive Branch's handling of foreign relations.

Depending on the activity of the President, the Secretary of State either plays first or second role, but even his second is significant because more normal and less hinged to crisis. Unlike the Chief Executive, he goes to "the Hill" for intimate briefings. He testifies in some detail not only on policies but specific legislation. Like the Chief Executive, he has legislative leaders to his office. Under Dean Rusk, a special effort has been made to introduce newly-elected Congressmen to the labyrinths of the Department. Also, the Secretary's wife has come to play an active role in familiarizing wives of Congressmen new and old with the Department and its workings.

A Secretary of great Congressional experience can do much along these lines. With personal and political connections he can enlist the aid of former colleagues. Relationships can be a bit smoother, the worlds can be made to overlap a little further. But so far, nothing has permanently reduced the magnitude of the problem or averted the annual appropriations catastrophe.

Institutional efforts made by State to connect the two worlds have been addressed principally to routine, day-to-day measures. To be sure, these measures have been directed at a fairly wide range of smaller matters, and State has pursued them sincerely. Over the years, they have helped somewhat to improve relations. But only occasionally have they had any real political impact.

Among the institutional devices to assist in a daily healing of the breach the Department belatedly established the position of Assistant Secretary for Congressional Relations. This office could be, and on some rare occasions has been, of great use, particularly when either former Congressmen, or former staff assistants to Congressmen or to Congressional committees have been appointed to it. But when occupied by men of little or no experience on "the Hill" or in the Department, it has been a prisoner of the Department and its attitudes. All too often the office has operated in routine fashion, performing only routine services, simply making sure that Congressmen's inquiries are answered as fully and promptly as possible and the legislators provided material requested by their constituents.

This service is commendable. It must be performed. But it is only a very small part of the job that needs to be done. When Congressman Rooney recently grunted at an Assistant Secretary, "Do you think Congressional relations have improved?" and the hapless official cautiously replied he thought, "They are about the same," Rooney snapped, "Just as bad, except you get out a lot of expensive publications and things." When the same hapless official was asked why he was requesting an increase of funds, and he replied "I do not know," Rooney was handed on a silver platter an instance of inexcusable ignorance which reinforced only too well Congressional doubts about the Department. It is hard to get funds for a department whose representatives do not know why they are needed.

For years the Office of Congressional Relations was staffed by civil servants. This provided continuity of experience, but did not bring the pyramidal diplomatic mass any closer to Congress. The quality of the diplomatic officers, their lack of political experience, their unfamiliarity with "the Hill," and their fetish of rotation militated against their use in the Office but their disinclination was also evident. Few wanted to risk their promotion chances with such responsibilities. So over the years the Office failed to improve one of the aspects of the Department's relations with "the Hill" most in need of improvement. Now, however, the office is a normal billet for rotating diplomats.

In other ways efforts have been undertaken to make the diplomatic establishment a little more visible to Congress and a little more responsive to Congressional thinking. In recent years, the Senate Foreign Relations Committee has invited a representative number of newly commissioned Foreign Service officers to appear before it for a friendly exchange of questions and answers. A sprinkling of new officers is assigned to Congressmen's offices for a period of a week or two to get a little familiarity with the ways of Congressmen. It has even been known in recent years for the Department to dispatch to a committee hearing a very junior diplomatic officer just back from a critical area to answer questions the Department-based officers could not so adequately answer. Congressmen are occasionally invited to address seminars offered by the Foreign Service Institute. And they sometimes attend the concluding ceremonies of its courses.

From time to time, State has recruited staff from "the Hill," not only for the position of Assistant Secretary for Congressional Relations, but also for other offices — often administrative, because of Congressional dissatisfaction with Departmental performance in that area. Congressman (now Senator) Thruston Morton has served as Assistant Secretary for Congressional Relations, Senator Walter George and Representative James Richards as special advisers to the Secretary, Representative Chester Merrow as an official in the Bureau of Public Affairs. From the staffs of Congressmen and committee has come an equally noticeable and sporadic siphoning of personnel — John Peurifoy, Jack McFall, Scott McCleod, William Macomber, Francis Wilcox — many of whom seek and later receive appointments as ambassadors, which has not endeared them to the diplomatic establishment. Nor have their general attitudes always done so. McCleod, for one, ridiculed young officers as "babies," reported back to a Congressional Committee that the Department's security operations were "chaotic," and urged stricter, more stringent tests "all along the line; first to qualify for the Service; a very hard-headed training period; not perhaps like our service academies, but certainly something to indoctrinate these people not only with what we hope would become the traditions of the

Service, but also the traditions of our country, and then a very strict, tough discipline to make sure that malfunctions and mistakes and wrong decisions and so on are not condoned; that a person who demonstrates that he does not have good judgment is not promoted, but is either put in a place where he cannot hurt you, or else dismissed from the Service."

A few Department of State civil servants and young Foreign Service officers have found lodgment on the staffs of Congressmen and Congressional committees. While the effect of this two-way migration has been to infuse some needed political instinct into the establishment and allay some Congressional distrust, it has also provided additional pipelines to Congress of State Department inadequacy. In any case it has effected no basic change.

One of State's techniques of collaboration is to invite Congressmen to serve on delegations in international conferences. This has helped improve relations and increased Congressional familiarity with foreign policies and diplomacy. It has also induced Congressmen to make more discreet and moderate statements. It has promoted bipartisanship, for representatives of both parties are invariably included. To the extent that lower-echelon officers have been in the delegations, an additional liaison has been effected between them and Congress. But lack of funds and staff has generally precluded the participation of young officers on an extensive scale.

A far more fundamental approach is needed to State's Congressional problem. Profound changes will not be accomplished by a mere smoothing of daily relationships. Nor will they be achieved by hard-pressed exertions of Presidents and Secretaries of State. They demand an exertion throughout the ranks of the career Departmental officers. More politically experienced people must be recruited, and more education in Congressional relationships provided. A study program in American politics must be instituted to keep every officer up to date with Congressional problems and more politicking on "the Hill" must be undertaken, especially with reference to appropriations. Above all, the Department must improve its substantive and administrative performance and send to "the Hill," to explain and defend its decisions, representatives who are well-informed.

One important aspect of the Department's relations with Congress has been particularly neglected — its service to Congress and, through Congress, to the nation itself. Let me illustrate the point this way.

I once asked a highly successful labor lobbyist the source of her success on "the Hill." She is an intelligent and dynamic person — but so are many lobbyists. She was so successful, however, and enjoyed such respect on "the Hill" that I was curious to know her particular approach. She put it this way: "I assume a Congressman is like me. I assume he would vote for the things I believe in if he could — if he understood them, if his constituents understood them so that his vote would not provide his opponents with a weapon by which to defeat him. So my task as a lobbyist is twofold: to have all the facts at my command which I would demand if I were in his place and to help him prepare his district for the vote I want from him. This means other things. I must readily admit my ignorance when he asks me a question I can't answer and go research the answer for him. It also means I must prepare material for him to get back to his constituents and myself visit his district if he wants me to, to make speeches, see editors, go on radio programs — do anything required to help educate the voters. This takes time. It takes funds. Above all it takes putting myself in the Congressman's position and working quietly — making a sincere effort — to help *him*. High-pressure tactics are out as far as I am concerned. The sell must be a soft sell. The sell must be service. For my interest is not simply to get one vote on one particular pressing bill and to leave a Congressman to sink or swim thereafter as best he can. What I am after in each case is an understanding Congressman elected again and again. So I help in his district as well as in Washington."

As I listened I marveled at what the State Department could do with this political realism. "I assume a Congressman is like me." If there is one thing diplomatic officers do not assume it is that Congressmen are like them. If there is another thing they do not assume it is that Congressmen would vote *their* way if they understood the issues. If there is one thing a diplomatic officer finds hard to admit it is ignorance. If there is one thing that annoys him it is a Congressman's request for information that takes appreciable time from his busy day. If there is one thing that never occurs to him to do, it is to prepare material for a Congressman's constituents, visit his district, sound out the people and work at the grass-roots level for the support the Department needs from that Congressman and his constituents. "I must have all the facts at my command." But when State Department officers go before the House Subcommittee on Appropriations they often do not have the facts. "The sell must be service." This the Department has never been politically sophisticated enough to learn. "To help him prepare his district for the vote I want from him." This carries us forward to a consideration of the Department's public relations.

CHAPTER 10

On Winning Friends
and Influencing People

In a democracy there must obviously be some official agency charged with keeping the public informed about our foreign policies and diplomacy. This responsibility belongs to the State Department. Let us examine how well it is discharged.

Informing, educating and influencing the public must start with an effort to learn what its opinions are. One must continually try to find out what people know and do not know, what their prejudices are, and where they are getting their information and misinformation.

The Bureau of Public Affairs uses four methods to do this: (1) a systematic scanning of current publications and public opinion polls; (2) an analysis of letters written to the Department; (3) liaison with citizens' organizations and other groups interested in public affairs; (4) informal contacts between individual Department officials and the public.

One office of the bureau reads the editorials, columns and feature articles of numerous daily newspapers, representing all shades of political opinion, as well as the *Congressional Record*, the findings of pollsters, magazines and periodicals, transcripts of television and radio comment, statements of political, business, labor and other leaders, and the resolutions of the more important private organizations.

Another office of the bureau reads the mail addressed to the Department, as well as some on foreign affairs directed to the President. The flow is, of course, irregular, increasing and decreasing according to the seriousness of policies and crises, but the stream is always there. Letters of Congressmen fall into a somewhat different category, for they are addressed to the Assistant Secretary for Congressional Relations and routed by him to the relevant political and economic bureaus for reply; but while they do not form part of the reckoning of public opinion by the Bureau of Public Affairs, they encourage an awareness of that opinion in other offices of the Department.

To the extent its limited staff permits, the Department pays special attention to communications from citizens' organizations. When a large, influential group sends in a query or resolution dealing with foreign policy, the document is often duplicated and circulated throughout the Department. The bureau may supplement these gratuitous expressions by soundings of its own, taken by public affairs officers dispatched to the national conventions of the more important organizations.

The Department is assisted in all this by the personal contacts of all its officers in their speech-making and social activities. Citizens serving the Department as consultants help to keep it informed on public attitudes, as do those few who serve on the panels for the selection and promotion of the diplomatic officers and inspection of overseas posts. Newsmen in search of information often give the Department clues to public opinion, if in no other way than by their questions. Exchanges with Congressmen at public hearings and informal gatherings provide additional sources. In this welter of opinions, individual and public attitudes must be distinguished.

Daily and weekly summaries of the bureau's gleanings, as well as special reports of opinion on particularly crucial subjects, are circulated throughout the Department, as well as to American delegates to international conferences and posts abroad.

In little of this activity does the bureau seek the cooperation of either universities and their institutes of public opinion or of foundations. Its own staff is limited in size, and its political instincts and depth of interest are not great. It is given no long-range chart by the policy planning staff by which it might gain long-range insight into areas of public ignorance and determine their relative importance. The bureau's quality of inquiry and analysis therefore leaves much to be desired. This deficiency (in addition to the psychological attitudes of the diplomatic officers, the pressure of work, and the lack of time for reading) causes other bureaus to pay little attention to these intelligence reports, however widely circulated they may be. In practice, the rest of the establishment is more influenced by its own attitudes, its own scanning of newspapers, and its own individual contacts, than by mimeographed reports on public opinion.

In informing and influencing the public three principal media are used by the Department: the usual mass media (newspapers, television, radio and magazines); the Department's own publications; and speeches by its officers.

The mass media have seen to it that their daily needs are

comparatively well served by the Department. In order to survive, a newspaper must be read, and a television or radio program must be heard. However often a Secretary of State holds a press conference — once or twice a week or only sporadically, depending on his tastes, the time at his disposal and the movement of events — he designates a subordinate to brief the mass media regularly. At noon each day, this official, having spent the morning collecting and confirming information and views on questions he expects to be asked, meets the media representatives.

Longer-range assistance to magazine writers and scholars not preoccupied with day-to-day news is rendered by a special staff of the bureau, supplemented by the Historical Office.

Apart from such formal channels, correspondents seek news, authoritative background information, and tips about things to come by talking privately with various officials of the Department, high and low. Secretaries of State have been known to make themselves frequently available to select correspondents. These chosen few and their confreres also gain access individually to other high officers of the Department at infrequent intervals. However, they also do a good deal of poking at every level of the Department in their search for inside information. Obviously, the attitudes of diplomatic officers and the pressures on them, as well as the necessity of guarding secrets, place great restrictions upon what can be obtained for public edification. As has been said:

> Most Department officials are overburdened with other duties; the function of giving out information has not been formally delegated to them, and when they talk with newsmen it is usually on their own time. One such official recently

remarked to the writer: "I've been meeting with reporters from time to time as a personal favor; it's not part of my job. But when I'm tired at the end of the day and want to go home and rest, they act insulted because I won't talk to them."

One can sympathize to a certain extent with this reaction. Moreover, a certain amount of caution in dispensing information is, of course, essential. But excessive caution and downright evasion are sometimes induced by the extravagant ambition for promotion and are always detrimental to the Department's public relations effort.

As to publications, the Department issues, in addition to daily press releases, many pamphlets and booklets setting forth texts of speeches by its officials, important diplomatic documents, and official studies and reports. These provide sound information, but they make difficult reading and are of limited popularity. Their solid, if *ex partes*, information is used by those with a special interest in foreign affairs — writers of background articles, teachers, students, special study groups. The same is true of its weekly magazine, *The Department of State Bulletin*, which reports many of the nonconfidential activities of the Department, but so dryly as to greatly limit its circulation. Furthermore, it leaves so much unsaid that it is not always illuminating. The new and more readable *News Letter* serves admirably as a house organ but requires great familiarity with the establishment.

Finally, there are give-away leaflets, "fact sheets," and the like, largely descriptive and unpolitical, which present material readily obtainable from encyclopedias. These brochures appear directed to the high school level of intelligence and certainly not to the more informed minds of the general public. The regular contact which the Department maintains with several hundred national citizens' organizations, with a combined membership of millions, provides one of the more systematic outlets for these materials.

To this literary output the Department has endeavored, in sporadic bursts of effort since 1944, to add programs of oral communication. Beginning in 1962, it has presented on three mornings a week, in its small auditorium in Washington, a public lecture, the advertised descriptions of which betray confusion in Departmental minds as to what exactly the lectures should cover and what part or parts of the public they are to serve. It has generally been publicized as a lecture on "foreign policy" but has in fact avoided that broad and complex area in favor of safer and simpler presentations of "how the Department works." As far as I know, these sessions have never dealt with diplomacy itself. They are often sparsely attended.

Almost any organization with a direct interest in foreign affairs can arrange for special briefing in the Department on particular subjects or geographical areas. An organization of high school teachers of a nearby county, for example, can arrange for a briefing on our Latin American, Asian or African policies.

Since 1961, the Department has annually invited to Washington representatives of the citizens' organizations with which it maintains contact for a "National Conference on United States Foreign Policy." It holds a similar conference semiannually for representatives of mass media from all over the nation.

Outside the Capital, the Department sends speakers to various important organizations and in recent years has supplemented the single-speech technique with one-day conferences on foreign policy in larger cities and, in smaller cities and towns, with several-day community-wide briefings which not only provide more give-and-take than the other programs but are available to more groups of a local, grass-roots character. Staff time and funds do not permit many of these. Nor do these limiting factors permit more than an extremely restricted use of another technique: posting diplomatic officers in universities for an entire academic year to broaden their horizons and make them available throughout their locality for talks. Diplomatic officers returning from abroad are encouraged to use a part of their home leave making speeches, but as Departmental funds available for travel expenses are limited and these officers have much family business to transact during these restricted periods, this technique has never been developed intensively.

Notwithstanding the apparent variety of these enterprises, the Department is under continual fire for the inadequacy of its public relations and information. Some of this criticism is generated by circumstances over which the Department has no control; some by governable elements of the Department's performance. It is the latter I shall deal with.

The three large categories of the Department's public may be said to be the "general public," the elite public and the publics of special interest. The general public demands to be kept as well informed as possible of current world developments, their significance to the nation, and the policies adopted and steps taken by our government to keep things moving our way. Its daily interests are such that only the more dramatic events get its attention; yet, if not forewarned of these, it is prompt to vent its long-smoldering distrust of the diplomatic establishment. It is not as emotional a public as can be found in some other countries, but all the same it is sensitive to reactions abroad and disconcerted by adversity in our foreign relations. It is in many respects remarkably well informed regarding the general contours of our foreign relations. Diplomatic officers who encounter this "general public" in their all too occasional contacts are invariably surprised by the extent of its familiarity with world affairs. While this public has sizable areas of ignorance and none greater than that of diplomacy itself, it is the source of a large part of the idealism underlying our Good Neighbor policy and our foreign aid programs.

At the other end of the spectrum is the elite, analytical public, which makes a conscious effort to keep abreast of foreign affairs and has a fairly good preparation for the purpose. It is a public ranging from college to business communities, to publishing and broadcasting circles, to professions and organizations having "foreign affairs" programs. It is an alert and articulate public, not without its representatives in Congress. Some parts of it have research staffs, and even lobbyists in Washington. It is the public that both produces and reads books, articles, editorials, and Letters to the Editor on foreign affairs; gives and attends lectures; invites the State Department to provide conferences and briefings. It is the public which sends its representatives to the Department's annual "National Conference on United States Foreign Policy" and the semiannual sessions for newspaper editors, radio and TV reporters from the fifty States of the Union. It is the public that assists in "Community Services to International Visitors" and, along with the general public, participates in many programs like "Experiment in International Living," "Hope," trans-national community improvement projects, Sister Towns, Sister Cities, Sister Schools, and the like. Its organizations are often affiliated with private international organizations which themselves hold international conferences, seminars and workshops. It is the public from which the State Department appoints advisers and consultants to itself, public members of its examining and promotion panels for diplomatic officers, delegates to intergovernmental conferences and many of our politically appointed ambassadors and Departmental officials. The elite also provides the Fulbright scholars. It enjoys a vascular system of international information, experience and insight far exceeding anything the State Department provides it.

Not even this public, however, has a sophisticated conception of diplomacy. It has only superficial impressions of the techniques of international relations. One of its members who had served overseas with our aid program once demanded of me: "Diplomacy? What's diplomacy but economic aid? If you haven't cash or something tangible to offer, what do you have to bargain with?" Neither he nor most other members of the elite know. A disastrously high proportion of them shares with the general public the idea that our world leadership depends simply upon our economic and military resources. The contribution to world leadership of the statesman of a small country like Belgium or that of the Talleyrand of a defeated power without aid or army is not sufficiently appreciated, if indeed, it is recognized at all.

Besides the general and elite publics, there are an infinite number of special interest groups or "publics." Some of these, such as the business, financial and publishing worlds shade off into the elite public, but principally the special interest pub-lics become involved in foreign affairs because of occupational interests rather than intellectual curiosity. They are less con-cerned with educating themselves in foreign affairs than in pressing upon the government their own special demands. They look to departments of the government other than State alone for information and assistance: to Commerce, Labor, Agriculture, Interior, the Treasury, Defense, the Fed-eral Aviation Agency, and a whole raft of offices closer to their special needs and more liable to give them the technical infor-mation and action they seek. This is a sector which provides the State Department with the serious problem of distinguish-ing between public opinion and publicly expressed opinion, between the public interest and the interest of an economi-cally important or influential element of the public.

The Department has traditionally been closest to the elite public. This is the public which, for a century and a half, has provided the majority of its diplomatic officers and civil ser-vants. The bond has been a natural one, and over the years the elite has been consistently sympathetic toward the Depart-ment. It is also the one public whose support the Department has tended to take for granted.

Ironically, the elite is the public which has been increasingly critical of the Department in recent years. It has examined the Department more searchingly than ever before and al-though it is reluctant to express its dissatisfaction, for fear of playing into the hands of unthinking isolationists and right-wing or left-wing extremists, it has expressed more and more frequently the opinion that the Department is lagging far behind the times.

Several former Department officers as well as scholars and other interested parties outside the establishment have helped to introduce this new critical wave. Trenchant criticism has also come from the commissions appointed by successive Presidents and Secretaries of State to inquire into the weaknesses of the diplomatic establishment and from hearings and staff studies of Congressional committees. Relatively few officers are more than dimly aware of this trend. Few have the time to read the studies it has produced. When they encounter the phenomenon it is only peripherally and, since they are rarely able to comprehend its significance, they tend to dismiss the criticism as fragmentary and uninformed.

The Department has been of little assistance either in acquainting its officers with these growing expressions of public discontent or equipping them to deal with it. Smugness and lack of political instinct have operated to prevent its taking the needed initiatives. During my long years in the establishment I never saw a study of the public's critical attitudes ever circulated within the Department. The Foreign Service Institute has avoided analysis of such criticism in its orientation and training courses and all but the most temperate criticism has been eschewed by even the *Foreign Service Journal,* which is published by the officers themselves and is therefore a private publication.

What is worse is the fact that Department officials have taken steps to stifle criticism and suggestions of reform from the outside. In 1958 a staff member of a university center of international studies published a report on the Department and the Foreign Service. It was a sober, conscientious, scholarly appraisal. Its criticism was wholly moderate, supported by carefully researched facts and directed to constructive suggestions of improvements. It was still too much for the diplomatic fraternity. When its author revisited the Department a year and a half later to update the study, the office of the Deputy Under Secretary for Administration had passed the word not to talk to this individual. On calls at various offices, the author was advised that only the Deputy Under Secretary was available for information and when an appointment was accordingly made for an interview, this official, a senior, able, distinguished diplomat — the epitome of the establishment — spent the appointed hour not permitting a single question but conducting a soliloquy which nicely avoided all the needed facts and elucidation. It was a shocking demonstration of the fraternity's prevailing attitude toward a private, responsible citizen and the free society in which it is supposed to function.

Such attitudes have, in fact, determined the quality of much of the Department's public relations effort. An organization of high school teachers requested a briefing on African developments and our policies and programs on that continent. The presentation was incomplete and evasive. When asked what kind of information program the United States is conducting in that part of the world and what kind it ideally should conduct if greater funds and other resources were available, one of the senior participating officers, who shortly thereafter became an ambassador in Africa, advised the questioners to get their answers from the USIA. Information, cultural relations and propaganda may be an integral, indivisible part of our total diplomacy in this age but this officer either did not want to get involved or else he did not know enough to answer. His policy of "keeping one's nose clean" was rewarded by promotion to the direction of one of the more crucial African countries, where the Red Chinese were making one of their hardest drives for control.

Other examples could be taken from the Department's recruiting efforts, which are also a public relations exercise and demand a good deal of information and skill. For recruiting purposes the Department has depended heavily over the years on junior and mid-career officers. The CIA, on the other hand, has often gone as high as its second in command, the Deputy Director. As a result, the Department's spokesmen have often been found by students and professors to be timid, uninformed, and evasive, and by contrast, the CIA's representatives mature, well-informed, frank, responsive, and not about to suggest that answers should be sought from some other agency.

The Department's contacts with the public have been greatly broadened by the cultural exchange program initiated by Senator Fulbright. This was a fine opportunity for State to find out how private citizens were thinking about foreign affairs, simultaneously to educate them, and possibly even to develop a much needed constituency. Let one exchangee who has taken the trouble to put down his experience show how this opportunity has been all too often overlooked. This man had been the editor of a big city newspaper, an author, a college teacher of literature and an intelligence officer for five years during World War II. He was invited to spend three months speaking and exchanging ideas in India, Korea and the Philippines. He wanted to do the best job possible. He was fully worth the Department's time.

The Department, however, suggested he spend but a day in Washington for briefing before departure. Knowing little of the program and some of the areas he was to visit, he was perturbed. "How could they tell me in one day all that I needed to know about India, about Korea and the Philippines?" he asked himself. "They would need to explain their program and tell me my duties, for I was to be an official representative of the State Department and of our government, and there was much instruction that I needed." Nevertheless, one day it was and even that proved poor in quality:

> . . . In the morning a man talked with me for perhaps twenty minutes about Korea. In the afternoon a lady talked with me for half an hour about India. The conversations were pleasant, and they told me of their travels, remembering little happenings that made entertaining stories. They recommended famous sights and suggested the better hotels. That was all — and the Philippines was not mentioned.
>
> This was my briefing, my total preparation by the Department of State for a three-month stay in India and for visits to Korea and the Philippines. When I tried to find out more about my job and what I was supposed to do, no one seemed to be quite clear about it, and I came away from Washington with little understanding of my duties.

When his overseas adventure was over, still other countries having been added to his itinerary:

> I was excited about getting home again and was eager to land in Washington and begin my work there. There was so

much to tell them and I believed that I could be of some help to the Department of State in my report, letting them know what I had seen and heard in all these countries where I had been working for them.

I had already heard from the Department of State and I knew their plans: When you return to Washington, we should like to arrange a debriefing for you which would enable us to hear the experiences of your trip. What we have in mind is a general session in which you would give an informal talk summing up your experiences and impressions, to be followed by a question period. After this debriefing we would arrange personal interviews with people here for detailed discussions. If you can give us an advance notice of ten days to two weeks of your arrival date in Washington, we shall be most grateful.

I had given them the notice, and I knew that everything was all set for the general session and the interviews. I was grateful for another letter that I had received from the Department of State: We would like to express our deep gratitude for your recent contribution to the Department's cultural exchange program. It is no exaggeration to say that you have been one of our most outstanding Specialists. To illustrate this, we should like to quote from several reports we have received about you. Then they quoted from reports sent in by USIS officials in the different countries I had worked in, and the reports were generous; but all that was behind me now, and I was interested only in the job here in Washington, for I knew that they would want to hear what a man with my experience in the past nine months had to tell. Certainly I wanted to tell them everything that I could, anything at all that would help the Department of State in their planning of our country's association with other countries.

I came into my hotel and called the Department of State and let them know that I was here, on time and ready. When did they want to see me? They told me to call back the next morning.

I did and they said that if I had anything that I would like to do that day, I might as well go ahead and do it, and to call back the next morning.

I did, and they said for me to come on over and I could get my financial papers checked and my vouchers signed.

I did, and that day I talked with one woman for fifteen minutes about India, one man for perhaps ten minutes about Pakistan, and another man for about ten minutes about Iran. Their questions were the casual questions of small talk. Had I had a good time? Had I met their friends? How was the weather? Each of them received me because he had been instructed to receive me, and each of them was as courteous as possible; but I was interfering with their routine, and they kept eyeing the papers on their desks.

These three visits were my report, and this is the only report of any kind that I was asked for then, or have been asked for since, by the Department of State, after having represented them in Korea, the Philippines, India, Pakistan, Afghanistan, Iran, Lebanon, and Israel.

The letter about the general session, the debriefing, and so forth was never mentioned.

I couldn't understand any of this, for I was accustomed to a different way of doing things. During the war we in intelligence wanted to talk to every man who came back from anywhere. He might not have much to tell, he might not be a smart man or an observing man, but we still wanted to talk to him, to ask him questions. We were bound to get *something*, maybe only the smallest detail, but it could play its part in helping us understand what we were up against, and help us figure out how to plan what must be done, and work out a way of doing it.

I couldn't understand this passing up a man who had been traveling around the world, going into all kinds of countries, and eight of them for the State Department itself. But after I had talked to other Specialists, I found out that this is the way it is done, and that nobody had been interested enough to talk to them either.

"This is the way it is done." I have quoted extensively here to convey fully the impact of the Department's attitudes and procedures on a large number of people simply through the exchange program. This kind of reaction can undercut the best press conferences, speeches and other public relations efforts of the Secretary and his summit associates. It causes the public to take with a grain of salt the Department's proclamations about how well organized it is, how capable its staff, and how masterly its grasp and guidance of foreign affairs.

Not even the relations of the Department with the press are as good as they appear on the surface. To many journalists the officers of State are gun-shy, self-satisfied, convinced they know it all, and inclined to look for sinister undertones in the most innocuous of inquiries. With the summit, the journalists have generally good relations. With the pyramidal mass, they rarely do. As in all the other relations of the Department, the more chronic problems originate there.

One striking example of this occurred when the Department belatedly recognized the onrush of African developments by establishing a separate bureau of African affairs. It displayed an all too customary inability to command its best resources. Instead of filling the senior positions in the new bureau with officers who had gained experience in Africa, it selected officers at random. Then, with its usual keen sense of public relations, the Department put out a press release disclosing this fact. A newspaper reporter drew this to the attention of his editor, who found it more than he could stand and exploded in a caustic editorial.

Reaction in the Department was characteristic. Instead of conceding its error, it took offense. A very high temperature was generated and some very purple words expressed the Department's indignation over the obtuseness and general myopia of the author. "That reporter," swore the public affairs officer of the new bureau, who was a career foreign service officer, "will never get anything more from me." This is hardly an attitude calculated to win friends and influence people. Nor does it do justice to the spirit and needs of a democracy.

The inability of the Department to assert sustained intellectual leadership and its preoccupation with a day-to-day routine has been displayed in no area more clearly than in this one of public relations. Here, again, the Department has failed to take the long-range view and it therefore has failed to stimulate a public appreciation of the underlying importance of diplomacy in gaining the nation's objectives. This has had disastrous effects. It has forced the American public to place too much faith upon economic-technical aid and force. The majority of the people, unaware of what diplomacy is and left uneducated by the diplomatic establishment, see world leadership too largely in terms of economic and military resources.

The Department's failure in this respect has also contributed to an exaggerated emphasis upon policy and policy making. This has characterized even our scholars' approach to foreign relations. Policy has become the all-in-all. The execution of policy has been neglected. People tend to believe that if we just work on developing good policies, through good policy-making machinery, our nation's efforts at world leadership will be crowned with success. Whether the nation is good enough to get its policies accepted abroad — that's for somebody else to worry about. Just *who* has never been clear.

When World War I came to an end, our colleges stepped

into the political and intellectual vacuum left by the recession of Wilsonian leadership by introducing courses on international relations. Year by year, they graduated men and women with an exposure to the kind of world they were living in and its problems. Twenty years later these citizens provided the reservoir of understanding which Presidents tapped for support of an active, responsible foreign policy.

To make that policy effective required another big leap forward. We desperately needed widespread teaching of the diplomatic means of implementing policy. Here our colleges failed. After World War II few introduced courses in diplomacy. The needed stimulation should have come from the diplomats. However, far from seeing the broad, democratic need for such an educational effort, the Department did not perceive even its own immediate need. It had to be pressured by Congress into establishing a training institute for its officers. It then restricted that training to languages and routine consular and administrative chores. It slowly and grudgingly extended the scope of the training, but never so far as to include any searching analysis of diplomatic tactics and techniques.

The Department and the nation were for a few years spared critical pressures demanding a mastery of diplomacy. They were given a short breathing spell, for the economic reconstruction of Europe brought into play the relatively simple task of exposing our industrial and technological know-how to sophisticated societies. The know-how was there: we simply had to appropriate the funds and devise the procedures for making it available. The political and psychological consequences of this farsighted program deceived us. They seemed to indicate our possession of a resourcefulness to lead. But once Europe was back on its feet, we began to flounder. We had not used the breathing spell to analyze and master the basic art of worldwide leadership.

It has been a Congressional subcommittee — the one headed by Senator Jackson — which has examined for public benefit how we get our national security policies subscribed to and supported abroad. The warm response that this Congressional approach has evoked from the elite public indicates how long and avidly that public has been awaiting such an examination.

The State Department has the following obligations to the American people:

1. To report the facts — the facts of world developments that vitally affect the nation — and to do so methodically, systematically, independently of the pressures of the mass media, and including the long-range trends which the public must sooner or later face squarely.

2. To define objectives. These must be clearly stated and understood by the public, and not on a crash basis, when crisis comes, so that the public unexpectedly has thrown at it an undigested "Truman doctrine," "Eisenhower doctrine," or "Johnson doctrine." Objectives must be defined in such time as to permit public examination and debate before periods of crisis make "unpatriotic" or "un-American" any question, even of the proposed objective, much less of the principle and tactics involved.

3. To state clearly and often the principles by which we should be guided in seeking our objectives. An informed public must have some manual of navigational principles. It cannot be merely an ignorant, garrulous, querulous passenger,

whose fate is dictated by a few experts — who may not be experts after all, but mere improvisers.

4. To clarify the means — the diplomacy — by which principles can be successfully applied to the winning of objectives.

5. With the foregoing, the Department must provide the needed interpretation, the needed historical perspective, the needed analysis. The facts, the objectives, the going principles, the art and means of leadership are not sufficient. The public must not only be informed, it must be educated. The State Department cannot relegate this task, as it once could, to the scholars, the historians, the philosophers. Crises are upon us today and others will arrive tomorrow. Decisions must be made and the public informed and prepared today — not next year, not simply over the next ten or twenty years.

We thus approach the fine line between information and propaganda. Our freedom depends on that line being kept clearly and conscientiously in mind, and therefore on the thorough training of State Department officers in the drawing of this line. In a democracy the people themselves must make or support the vital decisions without being hoodwinked or simply pressured to do so. To be sure, there must be popular persuasion by a democracy's diplomatic establishment, for there can be no leadership without persuasion. But leadership can lead to the ruin of a democracy if persuasion substitutes for information and education.

Such education of the public demands the highest capacity, the best education and training of officers that we can provide; it also requires the most favorable conditions of service and first-rate operating procedures. An overly cautious, superficially trained staff cannot instruct the people. No adequate presentation of issues can come from officers who are mesmerized by daily chores. It cannot come from a Department whose staff is so limited and poorly distributed that its best officers are the most hard pressed and become "bone-tired." It cannot come from a Department whose operating principles produce superficial generalists who fail to think about long-term goals, and who are denied the opportunity of committing themselves to these goals if they should happen to see them. It cannot come from men whose interest is narrowly focused on the next promotion list, men reluctant to brief anybody — whether a colleague, newsman, overseas lecturer or high school teacher — save the superiors who will write their efficiency reports.

This is where the Department stands, and this became sharply visible in the Vietnam crisis. Not until 1964, after long months of crisis, and only then under pressure of widespread public criticism, did it begin seriously to report the facts, define objectives, state clearly the principles it considered involved and provide some measure of analysis. Only when "teach-ins" evolved did it consider the academic community deserving of a serious program of speeches and lectures. Then, so long had it indulged the broad, optimistic generalizations of the defense establishment, State found itself involved in a crisis of its own — a credibility crisis. Its long-delayed elucidation simply was not believed by broad sectors of the American public. When the Department learns it must think and act in advance of crises it will not only improve its overseas performance; it will improve its performance at home and receive greater sympathy and support from the public it all too easily condemns as inadequately informed. One of these days, it is hoped, State will realize that one of the factors in the public's lag is its own.

CHAPTER 11

The Current Spurt

THE DEPARTMENT is capable of spurts of improvement. It is engaged in one now. As we have seen, some of the improvements to which reference has been made have occurred in recent years, many since 1961.

How far-reaching is the current flash of effort? How lasting will it be? Will its impact upon the quality of performance be more durable than that of earlier ones? Or will it, like the others, dwindle away, dissipated by the effects of personnel rotation and conservative attitudes?

Let us analyze the nature of the current leap forward and the changes it has introduced, for these can help answer such questions. The changes fall into seven categories: (1) Departmental leadership; (2) tone of performance; (3) organization and procedures; (4) administrative capability; (5) training, (6) the relations of the Department with other parts of the Federal establishment; and (7) public relations.

LEADERSHIP

The Department has seldom been visited by so long a period of change in its politically appointed leadership. The mystifying round of Presidential appointments, which began with President Kennedy's inauguration, has yet to cease. Neither of the two Presidents since 1961 has evidenced to the Department's satisfaction that he understands what qualities and experience it needs and possesses. This has led to bewilderment in the Department and a shaky morale.

Eighteen uneasy months led to Chester Bowles's replacement by George Ball as Under Secretary. The post of Under Secretary for Economic Affairs which Ball vacated was converted into one for political affairs and given to George Mc-Ghee. McGhee's vacated post as head of the policy planning staff was given to Walt W. Rostow, who had been serving at the White House.

McGhee's assignment did not work out and sixteen months later he was shifted abroad as ambassador to West Germany, replaced in the Department by Averell Harriman who was in turn replaced in 1965 by Thomas Mann, the position then being reconverted to one of economic affairs. With Mann taking over the top level economic problems, Ball shifted his attention to political and general relief of the Secretary. Harriman became a roving trouble shooter. But Mann resigned in 1966 and in the same year Rostow was returned to the White House, some of his functions at State being entrusted to a career man, Henry D. Owen, who became chairman of the Policy Planning Council, and others to Robert R. Bowie, who was named Counselor of the Department.

While these shifts were occurring at the summit, the pyramidal mass was inflicted with an even greater instability. We have already noted the protracted disturbances in the Latin American bureau, and all we need observe at this point is that in six years the position of Assistant Secretary for Inter-

American Affairs acquired five incumbents. The position of Assistant Secretary for Congressional Relations changed hands four times, as did those of Assistant Secretary for Public Affairs, for Educational and Cultural Affairs, and for Far Eastern Affairs. The Assistant Secretary for Economic Affairs was changed three times; the Assistant Secretary for Intelligence and Research, twice. The first coordinator of international labor affairs proved neither versed nor interested in his responsibilities and was replaced after two years of lost time.

At the same time, the lower echelons continued their frenzied rotation unabated. Deputy Assistant Secretaries came and went, as did office directors, deputy office directors and country desk officers, with an organizational switch from country desk officers to country directors superimposed upon this milling in 1966.

As a part of all this disrupting change in personnel occurred the Kennedy Administration's experimentation with the Department's top administrative post. Never stopping to examine what that post involved and whether it should be converted into a managerial position, the White House twice vainly sought an effective appointee outside the diplomatic establishment. First to serve as Deputy Under Secretary for Administration was a former chairman of the Civil Service Commission. If the diplomatic establishment were comparable in most respects to the rest of the Federal Government this would have been a stroke of genius, but it isn't and the outstanding Civil Service Commissioner, neither familiar with foreign policy and diplomacy nor accustomed to the subtleties of the Department's traditional ways of making its somewhat chaotic organization work, fell by the wayside.

The next appointment was even more difficult to rationalize, that of an attorney of the Department of Justice. He was equally uninitiated. After spending considerable time and hard-to-spare funds in overseas travel to overcome this deficiency, he was transferred back to Justice, the President evidently deciding he could be more useful as an Assistant Attorney General in charge of antitrust activities than in the diplomatic establishment. The White House then turned to the establishment itself, promoting the Assistant Secretary for Administration, William J. Crockett.

Crockett proved a good choice. He had had six years' overseas experience in administrative duties, first with the aid program, then with the Foreign Service. Earlier, he had had military, advertising and banking experience, as well as an overseas assignment with the U. S. Maritime Commission. Moreover, he was a quick, perceptive learner, interested in ideas and intellectually committed to improvement.

In the meanwhile, extensive overseas travel by all the political newcomers had prolonged the shakedown period. While critical of his predecessor's long absences from Washington, Secretary Rusk found himself spending some five of his first twenty-eight weeks in meetings abroad. SEATO, CENTO and NATO affairs, along with a Geneva conference on Laos and a foreign ministers' gathering in Paris, took him abroad for substantial periods. Under Secretary Bowles was frequently absent from Washington in efforts to stimulate public opinion at home and missions abroad. Harriman got pinned down in prolonged discussions overseas and the Assistant Secretary for African Affairs, unfamiliar with his new responsibilities, sortied to Africa three times in his first nine months of office, taking with him a retinue of subordinates. The President himself sallied across the Atlantic.

This current of travel was matched by another in reverse. A new Administration inevitably excites in other governments a desire to size it up at first hand and establish personal relationships as rapidly as possible. The competitive business of diplomacy demands this. Foreign visitors, accordingly, swept into Washington. At home as abroad the President, Secretary of State and other high-ranking officials had busy schedules of conferences with foreign leaders.

At the same time, the Department was faced by a great proliferation of nations, strapped for funds and bewildered by White House dissatisfaction with its performance. Faced by so many immediate problems, its pyramidal mass thought, in typical fashion, that the best it could do under the circumstances was to keep things moving from day to day. It scrounged for resources to meet current demands, reacted somewhat peevishly to White House prodding, trotted out its fire-fighting resources for daily brushfires and wondered why so many people felt it was failing to measure up to the nineteen sixties.

To this unfavorable situation the new Secretary applied himself doggedly. He had had earlier experience in the Department, having entered it in 1946 as assistant chief of a division, risen to office director and to Assistant Secretary for United Nations affairs, emerged in the summit entourage briefly as Deputy Under Secretary and reverted to the pyramidal mass as Assistant Secretary in charge of Far Eastern affairs. Like Acheson before him, he came to the direction of the Department knowing something of its ways and attitudes.

During the shuffling and shakedown of staff he acquired some steady associates. Ball proved an exceptionally able and steady *alter ego*. Apart from a year's service in Saigon as deputy ambassador, Alexis Johnson continued as Deputy Under Secretary for Political Affairs and pleaded with his career colleagues to cast off their traditional ways. Walt Rostow proved a steady rider as director of planning, as did Governor Williams and Phillips Talbott for African and Near Eastern affairs, respectively. Returning from Moscow in 1962 to retire, Llewllyn Thompson was persuaded to remain in service and proved a stable link with the Soviet ambassador in Washington as well as an able adviser on U.S.S.R. affairs to the Department and President. By the end of 1966, however, all these steady riders had vanished from State.

TONE

While riding out these changes, which brought mixed results, the Secretary endeavored with some success to counteract the decline in morale and elevate the tone of general performance. Coming into the establishment both in 1946 and 1961 as an "outsider," without fraternity connections or sensibilities, he made no pretense of being a "member"; at the same time he made it clear nothing could substitute for effective team play. He proved neither lone wolf nor runner with the pack, neither prima donna nor conformist. He began to show that his sole interest lay in advancing the substance and quality of American policy and diplomacy. He was unpontifical, unhistrionic, unconcerned with his place in history. He engaged in no tricks to preserve his status as head of the diplomatic establishment and adviser to the President; he never, for instance, kept information or decisions under his hat. Symbolically, he wore no hat.

Modest, sincere, highly intelligent, with an enormous capacity for lucid analysis, Rusk was early termed "a good technician." He was this and more. He understood the principles of democracy and a democratic approach to international affairs. He was concerned over our deficiencies in applying those principles at home and abroad. He was, moreover, profoundly ethical.

The Secretary thus gave to the Department a healthy tone: he suggested new attitudes, principles, and, to some extent, new operations. Simple and direct, he opposed the diplomatic officers' evasiveness. Modest, he challenged their smugness. Claiming no esoteric skill, he punctured their pretense of professionalism. Demanding fresh analysis at every turn, he disputed their conventional premises. Having a profound sense of unselfish service, he subtly shamed their own preoccupation with promotion. Far from being hypersensitive to criticism, he welcomed it and searched for its causes. When, in 1963, he invited the American Legion to "come and look us over," even Congressman Rooney was flabbergasted and admitted that this bespoke an entirely new attitude in the conventional Department.

The sincerity with which the Secretary emphasized quality of performance found expression in a number of ways, including the retention of a few experienced political appointees of the preceding Administration. William B. Macomber, Jr., for instance, had been with the CIA (1951–53), then successively special assistant to the Secretary of State (Dulles), administrative assistant to Senator John Sherman Cooper (Republican, Kentucky), special assistant to the Under Secretary of State (Herbert Hoover, Jr.) and then to the Secretary again, winding up in the Eisenhower Administration as Assistant Secretary of State for Congressional relations. He was retained by the Kennedy Administration, made an ambassador and subsequently assistant administrator of AID. Such an emphasis upon experience and quality regardless of political affiliation exemplified the clarity with which the new Administration grasped the need for a World Power to resist the loss of diplomatic leadership which comes with changes in the Presidency. It was part of the Kennedy-Rusk and Johnson-Rusk tone.

ORGANIZATION AND PROCEDURES

Unfortunately, much of the new tone appeared in improvements of daily operations rather than in basic changes. Some changes were reversions to earlier innovations. George Marshall's operations center, for instance, was restored at the summit to quicken and help systematize the Department's flagging follow-through. Other changes were entirely new. Two deputy assistant secretaries — one (as we have noted) for politico-military affairs and another for Atlantic affairs — improved the Department's daily relations with our military establishment and took up some slack in the handling of an increasingly knotty situation in our North Atlantic alliance. Alliance diplomacy, the Department finally conceded, could be as difficult as hostile diplomacy and indeed there were times when it was hard to distinguish between the two. Among the other innovations was an office of scientific affairs. A coordinator of international labor affairs was brought into existence, but this was largely a change in title, since a Departmental officer had performed this function since 1954; however, the position was now attached to the Secretary instead of a Deputy Under Secretary and men of trade union background were appointed to it.

One significant structural change, introduced largely at the initiative of the White House, placed the Latin American staff of AID (the backbone of our apparatus for developing the Alliance for Progress) in the State Department, side by side with the diplomatic officers dealing with Latin American affairs. This integrated the Alliance with the policies of the State Department, and State's diplomatic relations with our neighbors to the south began to change in fundamental ways. The inspired director of AID's Latin American staff, Teodoro Moscoso, had a large hand in this, and when he was replaced in 1963 by a career diplomat who was made at the same time Assistant Secretary of State for Inter-American affairs, another step was taken toward rational consolidation of our approaches to our Southern neighbors.

In some other ways, new notes were struck. The planning staff was invigorated, although it lacked the central influence it had acquired through the OCB. But it was at least relieved of suffocating operational minutiae and reinfused with intellectual talent from the outside. It threw a long-needed bridge to the military establishment by adding military officers to its staff. Planning advisers were assigned to the operating bureaus in a fresh effort to reduce the fatal gap between planning and doing. Country and regional planning, now severed from the rest of the government by the abolition of the OCB, was pursued independently of other departments. Internationally, two groups were formed, designed to improve the Department's international planning performance. The director of planning was made a member of both — the Inter-American Committee for the Alliance for Progress and the Atlantic Policy Advisory Group of NATO. Behind all this was Congressional prodding. Before Senator Jackson's subcommittee

Rusk acknowledged "we are in process of making a vigorous response to your verdict that 'a better planning effort is needed in State.' "

A single department's attempt to carry forward country and regional planning through national policy papers was bound to proceed slowly. It took almost four years of patient effort to complete a handful of these papers, and naturally the earlier of them were by this time out of date. Still, this effort sparked a significant contribution from the administrative side, of which we will speak later.

Like planning, research was invigorated. Its staff emerged more and more as a contributor not only to the thinking of both summit and pyramidal mass, but also to the Department's public relations. Although handicapped by limited funds, an effort was made to exploit resources outside the Department, extending not only to universities and foundations in the United States but abroad, where materials of great interest are being produced. Diplomatic officers were increasingly assigned to the research bureau in order to acquire an understanding of its practical importance. To confer prestige on such assignments, a few of the more outstanding assignees were promoted to ambassadorships.

Careful observers, indeed, could detect a singular feature in this "new" merger of diplomatic and civil service personnel in the research area. In effect, what was happening was a reversion to the earlier organizational pattern of the Department itself. Like the Department prior to 1954, the research bureau now possessed a permanent civil service staff to which was increasingly grafted a rotating diplomatic staff, thus combining needed continuity and professionalism with overseas experience. As compared with the situation before 1954, there was a change in attitudes: the permanent staff was just a little less scornful of the diplomats' superficialities, because these were slowly diminishing, and the diplomats were picking up a little of the new tone brought by Rusk and his summit associates.

ADMINISTRATION

As the new tone became evident here and there through the Department, Rusk's insistence upon a reexamination of the administration of the establishment began to bear results. Crockett had already been at work on this as Assistant Secretary; once elevated to Deputy Under Secretary, he pushed vigorously for "new and enlarged concepts of operation and management," for "new and bold approaches to old problems." "We must not cling to the past for the past's sake," he insisted. "We must embrace change where change is rewarding. We must think creatively; we must produce new ideas to meet the new problems of a new age."

"Overwhelmed with work, pressured incessantly by policy problems that cannot wait and attacked by both Congress and the public," a Secretary of State once observed, "it is little wonder that the Department has shunted aside administrative problems." Wonder or not, administrative problems could no longer be postponed. Crockett set task forces and consultants to work searching large areas of operations for ways to speed up, economize and improve. Administration was decentralized, giving greater responsibility and elasticity to operations of posts abroad. Administrative paper work and personnel were reduced. Some thirteen consular posts abroad were closed. In the Office of Foreign Buildings, to which Rooney had taken frequent exception, 75 officers were released and twelve of the fifteen regional offices overseas were abolished. The funds saved were used to alleviate some of the personnel shortages in other bureaus, moderating ever so slightly the pinch of Congressional penury. What many operating officers had long considered "the dead hand of bureaucratic administration" was noticeably lifted.

Promotion procedures were sporadically relaxed, principally at Presidential bidding, making possible a few spot, out-of-line promotions for exceptional service. As in the research bureau so in the administrative: a few outstanding officers were elevated to ambassadorships to dignify their work. This move included officers on the staff of the Foreign Service Institute which had always been viewed by the diplomats as an unlikely spot to look for outstanding people. In line with Rusk's dictum that the Department needed more chiefs and fewer Indians, ambassadors were used down to the level of office directors and special assistants to Assistant Secretaries, challenging the tradition that ambassadors be given at least Assistant Secretary rank. In order to combat unhealthy attitudes further, ambassadors were warned that the old convention of "once an ambassador always an ambassador" was out. The test was to be quality of performance.

Nevertheless, some career officers appointed ambassadors proved so little competent to run embassies that they demoralized their staffs and weakened the Department's influence abroad. One of these so paralyzed his staff that an inspection team had to be dispatched from Washington to straighten out the situation. This was bad enough but the Department compounded its error of judgment by subsequently rewarding the officer with its highest title of "career ambassador."

As a means of testing performance, not only of ambassadors but of diplomatic officers generally, Crockett and his staff took on a managerial function. Pressed by Secretary McNamara's example in the Defense establishment, Crockett's staff took the laboriously evolved "national policy papers" and applied these as yardsticks to our embassies' programs and activities. As inadequacies were bound to be revealed by such close, systematic scrutiny, diplomatic officers of a conventional cast of mind were resistant to the process. Worse still, from their point of view, was having to explain and justify their performance to administrative officers, whom they considered mere dabblers in diplomacy. Moreover, they feared that this was but one more administrative effort to straitjacket the art of personal diplomacy. Confronted by profound resistance, the effort was slow to bear fruit. But it persisted nevertheless, pushed along by the momentum of the "national policy papers" and stimulated by management seminars which Crockett introduced. These seminars, for lack of funds, could be attended by only a relatively few senior officers, but at least these few were alerted to some of the advantages of a more systematic conduct of foreign affairs.

Even the efficiency report system was given another of its many reviews. The pendulum swung back to the earlier, abortive, demoralizing rule of denying officers the right to see these reports at their overseas posts, this being reserved for their return to Washington on periodic home leave. The hope was that evaluation might become more candid and informative. The need for this kind of evaluation was underlined by a further decision to divide each report into two parts, one of general portraiture, the other of completely frank appraisal, but the latter evaluation of himself no officer was permitted to see even in Washington, thereby reviving an old morale problem.

Basically missing in all this was a central, systematic approach, buttressed by thorough personnel research. The personnel office which Crockett had inherited he split up and scattered, thereby making impossible a well-coordinated, well-researched consideration of the Department's recruitment, selection, placement and promotion problems. For a large organization in the second half of the twentieth century this was extraordinary. But Crockett's problem was resistance to research and reform and he may well have embarked upon this scattering of staff in order to preclude a coalescence of opposition. If so, it was a case of officers' attitudes compounding the Department's problems.

A different type of challenge was exemplified by the "information explosion" which had for some years made heavy demands upon the Department. The diplomats' incapability of using the wealth of information and insight pouring in upon them both from colleagues overseas and from the vast research of scholars had become a serious problem. Limited in staff assistance by unduly restricted Congressional appropriations and handicapped by their own inadequate interest in modern computing systems, political and economic officers were spending more and more time on clerical and semiclerical duties, including indexing and filing.

Other departments and agencies concerned with national defense had spent millions of dollars analyzing this need, designing and installing new mechanized information systems.

Spectacular advances had been made even in such non-defense agencies as the Patent Office and National Library of Medicine. Among the agencies most critically affected, State had lagged behind badly, and even under the current spurt of improvement progress was lamentably slow.

This situation combined with other factors to produce embarrassing results. One of these factors was the effort to economize on filing cabinets and space. An administrative instruction was issued to restrict filed material to a five-year span. Thus, in 1966, no one in the State Department had at hand any record of any event, decision, policy or diplomatic move made in 1960 or before. Combined with the rotation of officers, this exposed American diplomacy to the certainty of endless miscalculations.

One of these flashed upon the front pages of the press around the world in August of 1965. When the prime minister of Singapore, Lee Kuan Yew, claimed that a $3.3 million bribe had been offered him five years before by the CIA, the State Department denied the charge. Lee produced a letter from Secretary Rusk apologizing for the incident. Only then, humiliated before the world, did the State Department ascertain the facts and admit the affair. The Department's explanation was that the officers who knew of it had been rotated somewhere else and those currently in charge of Singapore and Southeast Asian affairs knew nothing about it. This was a sad admission for the diplomatic establishment of a World Power.

Less spectacular but equally revealing of the Department's continuing difficulty in getting itself properly organized was an internal affair. Crockett's immediate predecessor, William P.

Orrick, had chanced to arrive in Bonn in 1962 on the heels of the peripatetic Congressman Rooney. Orrick's alert political sense prompted him to inquire what the Congressman had said and done. "Nothing," was the embassy's response. "But he must have looked at *something*," Orrick insisted. "Oh, yes," was the afterthought, "he looked at the train schedule." "Train schedule?" "Yes. The embassy's train." "Embassy train? Hmmm," said Orrick and took himself to the ambassador, a career diplomat, who explained that the train was inherited from the occupation period, when the army used it for troop recreation. Successive ambassadors had retained it for official trips to Berlin and other places and to provide embassy personnel transportation to the Bavarian Alps for diversion.

Neither the ambassador nor his staff lacked transportation. He himself had a government-provided Cadillac and chauffeur. He had an Air Attaché's plane at his disposal. He, and his staff, had access not only to German train service but U.S. military trains as well. Both the British and French ambassadors had given up their special trains. What was the point in the American ambassador keeping his, especially when it ate into the Department's sparse funds? Orrick left Bonn under the impression that the ambassador agreed to surrender the anomaly, but when he got back to Washington he found the Assistant Secretary for European affairs, also a career diplomat, extremely reluctant to part with the long-enjoyed frill. Either political instinct was missing or the intrusion of an administrative officer was resented — or both. Orrick warned of Rooney's interest in the subject. Still no budging. Not even a further warning at Rusk's budget review had any effect. Sure enough, Rooney was lying in wait. At the next hearing on the appropriation request of the Department he took the skin off its back. The train was promptly given up.

Why this could not have been done on ample warning by a politically conscious, highly placed officer will no doubt have become clear from our earlier discussion. Why it had not been done long before, simply as a matter of economy and common sense, may also be clear from what we have said. Why the Deputy Under Secretary for Administration — or the Secretary — could not have ordered the discontinuation of the train raises the question of effective management. So does the later decision to make the Assistant Secretary for European Affairs an ambassador.

Equally disconcerting from an administrative point of view was the continuing difficulty of the Department to achieve a reasonable level of security control. Old attitudes figured in this problem, as did the absence of an effective general manager. One official felt so strongly about the Department's decision to clear a controversial Foreign Service officer that he leaked his apprehensions to a Senate committee, thereby igniting a blaze which not only took much time of the President, the Secretary, the Deputy Under Secretary for Administration and other officials to check, but eventually consumed him. He was transferred to other work and, when he refused the transfer, was dismissed.

If this was a controversial affair, the results of an inquiry into the Department by the American Legion was not. Long distrustful of the diplomatic establishment, the Legion promised to surface at its 1963 convention a resolution requesting the President and Congress "to undertake a thorough review of the State Department in all its aspects, and to take all measures necessary to improve and to maintain at a high level the public confidence in this extremely vital agency." In his appearance before the convention, Rusk stated he welcomed investigation but, since the Department was always being "investigated" by Congressional committees, invited the Legion to undertake its own. The Legion accepted the proposal and its representatives "devoted a considerable number of crowded days to visiting State Department facilities both in Washington and at overseas posts." Their report was generally favorable, but one thing it discovered was that "the State Department building in Washington is operated as an ordinary public building, despite the many sensitive operations contained there . . . visitors are not stopped or questioned at points of entry except at night." A hostile operator, that is, could enter the Department freely during the day, stay overnight and leave the next morning undetected, with such information and documents as he might have been able to acquire. The Department acted promptly with measures designed to protect its building around the clock. But why had this not been done before? Why did it take an outside organization to put this elementary precaution into effect?

TRAINING

Obviously all these situations required a reexamination of training and an inquiry as to how it could be reorganized to instill greater vigilance in officers, to encourage their acceptance of the new criteria of performance, and to prepare them more adequately for the demands of a hard-pressed World Power. In this, the Department fell far short of the mark.

It dabbled with improvements. It brought to the Foreign Service Institute in 1962 the best director it had had for years — an experienced diplomatic officer with exceptional academic qualifications. With a Ph.D. from Harvard and teaching experience in philosophy, George Morgan had served in the army in World War II and then entered the Department. Later, he joined the Foreign Service as a War Manpower appointee — thereby avoiding parochial fraternal ties — took Russian language training and served in Moscow, Berlin and Tokyo, put in a stint with the Operations Coordinating Board and then with the Department's policy planning staff. Such credentials were good indeed for a training director. As usual, however, the Department made use of them for too short a time. In three years Morgan was rotated out. Although he had made improvements, he had had insufficient time to challenge old patterns of training. The Department even failed to meet the growing demand from Congress and from a wide variety of public groups for a worthy Foreign Affairs Academy, comparable in its own sphere to the military training facilities in theirs.

Some five and a half months elapsed between Morgan's rotation to the field and the swearing-in of his successor. The long delay was unfortunate and no doubt testified to the scarcity in the diplomatic establishment of officers imaginative and resourceful enough for this demanding job — and personally interested. When a new director was finally appointed toward the end of 1965, the Department went outside its active ranks and designated a retired career ambassador, George V. Allen. By this time there had emerged in the top ranks of the Institute two able career officers, one of whom had just spent a year at a leading university and acquired a vision of the advances in learning and educational techniques of the last quarter century. Under these three men the Institute began to come alive in long-neglected, substantive areas.

Political outsiders had already forced the breaking of new ground. From the White House and the Attorney General had come pressure for the training of officers to meet the communist threat of insurgency and guerrilla warfare. Then the Agency for International Development and CIA had demanded special training for their officers who would serve in Vietnam. Both forms of training were instituted but the Department itself just had not seen the need.

In fact, even as the Secretary was boasting before the Rooney subcommittee that he had asked for no personnel increases for five years, the pressures of overwork and the dead weight of conventional thinking were beginning to have an unhealthy effect upon the Department's whole concept of training and to contest the new leadership of the Institute. While every other profession, including the military, was intensifying training and education, the State Department was trying to turn back the clock. A strong reactionary trend set in. The period of general orientation of incoming officers, as we have noted, was reduced from eight to six weeks, and while four more weeks were required after an officer had served a tour abroad, none of this added up to true professional training. A specific need like economic training, could be appreciated by the narrowly pragmatic department, and in this field a twenty-two-week course was pioneered. But twenty-two weeks to give neophytes a thorough grounding in the history and government of their country, in foreign policy, international law and diplomacy? This was unthinkable. Even eight weeks were too many. Six were enough.

Mid-career training likewise suffered. The whole idea of consecutive weeks of training was discarded. One-week periods of exposure to various areas were substituted for the former twelve-week course. Even these shorter periods were objectionable to the senior officers presiding over the pyramidal mass and posts abroad. To resist this reactionary trend the Department revived a training advisory committee, consisting principally of deputy assistant secretaries, in the hope of enlisting greater cooperation from the bureaus in effecting release of the better mid-career officers for its one-week training doses. But basic attitudes and staff stringencies determined the immediate response of the bureaus. Even a week's absence from a desk was frowned upon. At least one-third of the applicants for each one-week course were refused permission to attend by their superiors. There were even complaints among older officers that mid-career officers were being "stirred up" to take the one-week courses.

RELATIONS WITH THE FEDERAL ESTABLISHMENT

The move to fill the vacuum left by the dismantling of the Operations Coordinating Board was a long time in coming and when it did come resulted from the pressure of a military officer and the President. During the interval the Department did little to provide the leadership within the Executive establishment that was urgently needed. On a limited scale, promising mergers occurred — that of State's and AID's staffs dealing with Latin American affairs and the USIA officer corps with the Foreign Service.

Congressional relations showed some improvement. With

the Secretary and Crockett taking a genuine interest in economy and efficiency, the Department made a slightly more favorable impression with the legislators. Congressmen could not fail to be impressed by the closing of consular posts and the reduction in staff of the Office of Foreign Buildings.

This advantage was followed up. Congressmen were occasionally invited to participate in training courses as speakers. Newly commissioned officers were taken to Capitol Hill for a one-day briefing by Congressmen, an experience so illuminating to recruits who barely knew how their National Legislature functioned that it led to the assignment of a few young officers to work for a week in Congressmen's offices. An occasional Foreign Service officer, responding to the new trend, visited his Congressman on his own initiative. This activity was really quite superficial, but it was so unusual that it was greatly publicized by the Department.

The proposal of a national academy for more effective training of diplomatic officers and other government officials dealing with foreign affairs came from Congress, but it petered out once hearings were concluded by the Senate Committee on Foreign Relations. This failure was caused by the inability of the Department to follow through, and the skeptical attitude of the committee chairman, Senator Fulbright.

In 1962 there occurred a significant development in State-Congressional relations — as well as State's public relations — when two high-ranking Department officials appeared as guests in the Congressional recording studios to answer Congressmen's questions. The recordings were then made available to broadcasting stations in the Congressmen's districts.

Relations with both Presidents during this period left much to be desired. By way of illustration, one might recall Arthur

Schlesinger's description of President Kennedy's reaction to the Department after some months of experience in the White House:

> . . . One muddle after another — the Department's acquiescence in the Bay of Pigs, the fecklessness of its recommendations after the disaster, the ordeal of trying to change its attitude toward Laos, the maddening delay over the answer to Khrushchev's aide-memoire and the banality of the result, the apparent impossibility of developing a negotiating position for Berlin left Kennedy with little doubt that the State Department was not an instrumentality fully and promptly responsive to Presidential purpose.
>
> He well understood the difficulty of converting a tradition-ridden bureaucracy into a mechanism of swift information and decision. But resistance was no less great in Defense, where McNamara was plainly making progress in annexing the Pentagon to the United States government. Other departments provided quick answers to presidential questions and quick action on presidential orders. It was a constant puzzle to Kennedy that the State Department remained so formless and impenetrable. He would say, "Damn it, Bundy and I get more done in one day in the White House than they do in six months in the State Department." Giving State an instruction, he remarked, snapping his fingers with impatience, is like dropping it in the dead-letter box. "They never have any ideas over there," he complained, "never come up with anything new." "The State Department is a bowl of jelly," he told Hugh Sidey of *Time* in the summer of 1961. "It's got all those people over there who are constantly smiling. I think we need to smile less and be tougher."

Some of this criticism was unfair to the Department. State is not strictly comparable to other departments, for it is deeply enmeshed in the policies and attitudes of foreign governments. Of course two people can move faster than ten or twenty. It is hardly true that its officers "are constantly smiling." But the President was fair in saying that the Department was slow, conventional, shallow in its ideas, resistant to fresh thinking. The need to get tough was certainly there and, first of all, with itself and its shallow, ambling attitudes.

PUBLIC RELATIONS

No Administration was more conscious of the need of improving the State Department's public relations than that of John F. Kennedy. We have noted Chester Bowles's concern with this as Under Secretary. It was shared by successive Assistant Secretaries for Public Affairs and Ernest K. Lindley, a newspaperman appointed as special assistant to Mr. Rusk. From these political appointees came the broadscaled effort described earlier to carry foreign policy to the people.

In specific areas, also, came resourceful effort. G. Mennen Williams, as Assistant Secretary for African Affairs, showed an acute sense of the need for and capability in developing better public relations in his particular area. Among other things, he formed a public committee advisory to his bureau. The scholars on this committee drew sorely needed learning and insights to the Department. As we have noted, the Bureau of Intelligence and Research was also exceptional in its efforts to reach for resources outside the Department but was handicapped by severe financial limitations.

More broadly, in late 1966, the Department moved to place itself in a position to extract ideas and advice somewhat more systematically from the elite public by extending the technique of public advisory groups. The extension was announced as including geographical bureaus, the Bureau of International Organizations Affairs, and the Policy Planning Council. This move came three years after the initiative of the business community to form a "Business Group for Latin America," which has served as a consultative panel for the Bureau of Inter-American Affairs, and the more representative public advisory committee which Williams created for the Bureau of African Affairs. While action along this line is commendable, the Department is betraying an all too customary disinclination to move rapidly. Moreover, the advisory panels announced at the time of this writing for the Bureaus of International Organizations Affairs and of East Asian and Pacific Affairs consist, unfortunately, primarily of former Departmental officers and supporters of the Administration's foreign policies. Noticeably absent from the panels are dissenters.

In adding "public" members to oral examination panels, promotion boards and roving inspection teams, Crockett brought to the Department fresh thinking in these areas and enlightened a few more "opinion leaders" on the establishment itself. But this still failed to retrieve ground lost during the McCarthy period. In 1946, a long dormant advisory committee on the selection of diplomatic officers had been revived and distinguished educators had been associated with it, including the presidents of Harvard and the University of Minnesota, as well as two former Under Secretaries of Commerce, personnel officers of several large corporations and others with particular competence in the techniques of examination and selection of personnel. In 1953, during the wave of anti-intellectualism associated with the name of Senator McCarthy, the whole system set up by this committee and operated under its supervision had been summarily destroyed "without even an attempt by those who carried out the work of destruction to understand just what it was they were destroying." This systematic approach, involving some of the best minds and most representative citizens of the nation, has never been revived. The Department has all but forgotten it ever existed.

By detailing a handful of officers to universities for an academic year, Crockett threw another slim, tenuous bridge across the gulf separating the Department from the community of learning. By refreshing and updating their own minds these officers created, among other things, a small reservoir which could be called upon to invigorate training. By their participation in classes, they could bring to the universities insights which practitioners alone can contribute. By engaging in public speaking to all kinds of community groups, they added to the Department's general public relations efforts. Unfortunately, this experiment has been limited, by financial and personnel stringencies, to very few officers.

A resourceful lady of newspaper and political experience, Mrs. Katie Louchheim, stimulated Foreign Service officers who were returning on home leave, to get out into the hinterlands on speech-making and image-building trips. Conceded by the more open-minded officers to be twenty years late and worthy of support, these efforts were strapped for funds. Only the donations of a private company and a foundation made available three trailers and tow-cars for the purpose — all too little, all too late.

Public relations and image-building in the end depend upon performance and performance depends in good part upon attitudes, operating procedures and managerial competence. Other factors are a staff of adequate size and funds to develop public relations. In none of these did the Department measure up.

VIETNAM

On no subject was all this more evident than Vietnam. This was one problem which the current spurt of improvement never reached. Since 1954, when the Geneva accords brought brief respite to Southeast Asia and the acknowledged unsteadiness of the agreements led Dulles to negotiate the formation of SEATO and to bring Vietnam within its defense perimeter, we have faced a critical need for special knowledge of the area and special skills to deal with its problems and anticipated crises. Marshall's comments about our general situation in 1947 apply equally well to 1954: we were beginning to play with fire in Southeast Asia and had all too little with which to put it out. The few resources we did have we permitted to be dissipated by rotation of officers and lack of good management. Moreover, for ten years after 1954 the Department introduced no profound training of officers for that area. It did not stop to analyze the new commitment. It did not ask itself what skills the new responsibilities demanded. When it finally moved, it moved too late, too late to lead — it could only react — and when it did move, as we have seen, it was not from its own recognition of the need, but from the pressure of two other agencies.

Such great carelessness is indeed disturbing, and its connection with deeply-rooted attitudes and procedures will be clear from our preceding analysis. But let us pursue Vietnam, picking up at 1957 rather than 1954, so as to give the Department three years to perceive the magnitude of the problem and adjust to it. From 1957 to 1963, the year in which Vietnam became a matter for the Secretary himself to handle, three different desk officers in the Department handled South Vietnamese affairs — one for considerably less than two years. Their immediate supervisors — directors and deputy directors of the Office of Southeast Asian Affairs — were also changed during this period: four of each came and went. Only two of the desk officers and one of their superiors had served in Vietnam, and these three relatively experienced men naturally had difficulty in making their knowledge prevail in the face of their colleagues' ignorance.

Once in possession of a little familiarity with Vietnam, officers were rotated elsewhere. Those serving one tour in the Department and one in our Saigon embassy were thereafter scattered all the way from Amman to Marseilles to Ougadougou. No cadre of specialists was developed until very recent years.

This travesty of diplomacy occurred not only in the Department's lower ranks, but in its upper ranks as well. The Department can sometimes, through a happy accident, have men in its upper ranks who have great experience and knowledge of a given country, while maintaining men in its lower ranks who are relatively uninformed about it. Unfortunately, this has not been true in the case of the Vietnam situation: all men, at high or low levels, who have been connected with that trouble spot have been rotated frequently and have been unable to acquire sufficient experience. In the eight-year period 1957-65, there have been six Assistant Secretaries of State for the Far

East and four different Deputy Assistant Secretaries for economic matters. Of these ten, six had had no experience in
Southeast Asia, and all but one had had none in Vietnam.
None had been given any special training in Vietnamese
affairs before or during their tenure of office.

During this same eight-year period we had three Secretaries
of State, five Under Secretaries, and three officials whose titles
varied from Under Secretary to Deputy Under Secretary for
Political Affairs. Two of these had had experience in Southeast Asia, but none in Vietnam.

This same disastrous situation prevailed in Saigon as well.
Officers were rotated in and out, barely able to understand
the complexities of Vietnam before departing on some other,
far-off assignment. Officers assigned there even failed to receive systematic briefings. Far too many of the embassy staff
were junior officers who were unable to impress Vietnamese
officials, because they were so young and inexperienced. During the entire period — until the special training on Vietnam
began in 1964 — only two officers serving in the embassy had
Vietnamese language training in their record. Few had had
any military training and the Department evidently made no
effort to expose them to military problems that might arise in
Vietnam. When the Department was finally pressured into
giving a counter-insurgency course in Washington, there was
but a feeble effort for a long time to put through the course
diplomatic officers who were under consideration for assignment to Saigon or to the Department's Office of Southeast
Asian Affairs.

The Department simply waited for trouble to start and dissipated its limited resources of men who had had some expo-

sure to Vietnam. It made no move until 1964 to develop a cadre of "Vietnam hands," in the way that early in this century we had developed specialists in China and Japan, and, since 1933, on the Soviet Union. The Department's outworn procedures and attitudes governed its approach to Vietnam, regardless of who was Secretary of State. The crisis gathered without the most elementary kinds of preparation.

This was not diplomacy. This was not leadership. This provided no effective "front line of defense" in Vietnam or Southeast Asia. When the Vietnam crisis broke in full fury at the end of 1963 we did not have the experts in Vietnamese psychology, religion and politics we desperately need for the influence we must wield. Until we acquire this expertise in an adequate number of officers and employ these officers consistently on Vietnamese affairs, it is well we have little influence, for influence without understanding can lead to disaster. This is a central problem the Department must face, and it clearly is failing to do so when it contracts, rather than expands, the education and training of diplomatic officers, neglects to moderate the rotation of officers and does not gear planning and research to training and assignments, so as to prepare officers adequately for the problems and crises which are beyond the day's horizon.

CHAPTER 12

By Way of
Conclusion

WHAT DOES all this add up to?

The new spurt of improvement has reached some areas of the State Department, challenging but hardly revising many attitudes and operating procedures, and plainly leaving untouched the heart of the problem — the effective application of resources to the foreign policy and diplomacy of a World Power. There are too many gaps in the Departmental organization, too many dangling ends in its operations, too many hard, basic problems that are being tinkered with rather than tackled with available national means. Planning is not adequately coordinated with training, which remains too much a week of this and two or three weeks of that, or to the assignment of officers; the recruitment of men, the development of their skills and the formation of their attitudes are insufficiently tailored to our needs and commitments abroad; and the Department is still not facing up to the fact that it is a large organization, with all the problems of a large organization.

Changes effected by the new spurt offer little assurance of being continued when the reformers pass on. The more durable political appointees at the summit sufficiently knowledgeable and interested to be considered supporters of reform began to be replaced in 1966. Those of career status, like Crockett and Alexis Johnson, are subject to rotation and indeed Johnson has been assigned as ambassador to Japan. Few reforms these able men have introduced have a prospect of permanence or of serving as a solid foundation for further advances.

One source of innovation promises to remain. This is what I call the new breed of diplomatic officer — a breed which has been entering the establishment since World War II. Indeed, under pressure of Congress over the past twenty-five years, the State Department has extended its recruitment efforts to all parts of the country, all income levels, all social strata. The candidates it examines represent every conceivable background. This is not an unmixed blessing, for it is only one of several functions of the diplomatic establishment to "represent" the United States. An important function, also, is to exert influence and win respect for the United States. If our foreign policies are to mean anything our representatives must be David Eugene Thompsons, Jules Jusserands, David Ormsby-Gores, Llewellyn Thompsons, Alexis Johnsons, Foy Kohlers, Edwin O. Reischauers. The effectiveness of foreign policy and diplomacy — we must continually remind ourselves — is not simply a matter of how good *we* perceive them to be but how good foreigners perceive them to be. So, too, with our diplomatic officers. They must be judged by that criterion also — they are not as good as *we*, but as foreigners think they are. History is full of examples, from the Delian League onward, of how leadership has been lost because of a failure to keep in mind this prerequisite of success.

A disconcerting weakness in the new breed is the superficiality of their preparation for a diplomatic career. Many of those who are now young officers were too busy earning pocket money in high school days, working their way through college, and engaging in extracurricular activities to read widely. Most of them, in fact, are abysmally ill read. They know too little of the history, government and Constitution of their own country to add to the knowledge of any well-read foreigner or to deal successfully with the President and Congress at home. Few have a foundation of knowledge of diplomacy on which to build a creative career. Few know anything of international law. Few have more than a hazy impression of the United Nations and the other international organizations to which we belong and of the commitments these involve. Few grasp the democratic way of life in a sound enough fashion to be able to articulate it clearly and persuasively. Many, indeed, have encountered in their own communities problems and compromises of democracy which leave them confused.

These limitations would not be so disturbing if the Department recognized their existence and set to work systematically to remove them. But it doesn't. It does this neither when it commissions officers nor at any other time during their careers. To take a correspondence course in international law, for instance, a diplomatic officer cannot apply to his own establishment. He must apply to the military. The diplomatic establishment in the mid 1960s — in a century which has seen great advances in adult education — has no correspondence courses of its own except in the technicalities of consular affairs.

Few of the new breed have had political experience prior to

their admission to the diplomatic establishment. Few understand the role of Congress and public opinion in our foreign policy and diplomacy. One can hardly expect very creative contributions from them in these areas. Finally, it is hard to keep the best of the new breed in the establishment. They encounter frequent opposition from the old-timers. They become disillusioned by Congressional and White House criticism and lack the depth of learning which would stimulate them to search for the causes of criticism and to find correctives. They experience many frustrations in their operations. They perceive that our diplomacy is not attuned to modern needs, being still "social rather than executive," too much "concerned with personal relations rather than with national and international problems," aiming at "patching up appearances rather than achieving long-run purposes," with a view to "playing for safety, and postponing or avoiding immediate trouble." They feel our diplomacy conforms too greatly to "familiar and orthodox formulas." Hence, the morale of the new breed is hard to maintain and some of its ablest, most promising officers drop out after one or two tours of duty abroad.

Two examples will throw some light upon this problem. One of the more promising of the new breed to enter the establishment in recent years had done graduate work in foreign affairs prior to entry. He lacked a sound knowledge of American history and culture, but could discuss intelligently our foreign policies and problems, the United Nations and international law. Not only did he have unusual breadth of knowledge in these areas, but he also had a first-class, analytical mind. After but one assignment — to a small embassy in

Africa — he resigned. Why? His answer was this: "I looked at my senior officers and I did not like what I saw. They were shallow, preoccupied with their personal futures, uninterested, really, in the problems of foreign policy or even in the Foreign Service save in those respects affecting them individually. If this is what happens to career people in this business, it isn't for me."

Another young officer recently admitted to the establishment had equally outstanding qualifications. When admitted to the Foreign Service, he was completing his education at Harvard. He had keen intellectual interests, good sense, initiative, drive and a real knowledge of diplomacy. He, too, lasted one assignment — to a consular post in Europe. Why did he quit? For the same reason. The old-timer who was in charge of his post and the lady consular officer who was his immediate supervisor impressed him as people of limited imagination and interests. The broad concerns of American foreign policy and diplomacy were beyond them. Accordingly, they had little interest in developing their staff and for two whole years let this young officer virtually wither on the vine. Their efficiency reports on him revealed nothing amiss. So, unless one knew the officer, the records of the establishment would have revealed to no personnel or administrative official the basic source of difficulty — that the junior and senior diplomatic-consular offices were living in different worlds and something had better be done to bridge them.

The prevailing reaction of the establishment to this phenomenon is that the rate of resignation among the new breed is not excessive. This overlooks two vital points: among the dropouts are first-class officers and the very conditions which frustrate them likewise frustrate those who remain. The real point at issue for the Department is not the durability, but the development of its officers, not the willingness of some to put up with discouraging conditions, but the ability and courage of the organization to remove those conditions.

Notwithstanding their serious limitations, the younger officers clearly have many strong points. They are alert, intelligent, unconventional, dissatisfied with things as they are. They do not share the old-timers' consuming predilection for the "artificial patter of the cocktail circuit." These are men who can mix with fishermen as well as financiers, with bricklayers as well as bankers. They know the outcast *mestizo* may be as important in the long run — although possibly not during their own particular assignments — as cabinet ministers. On home leave in the United States they are less inclined than their seniors to gather in familiar haunts and more inclined to get jobs reporting for small-town newspapers or picking apples in Virginia. They are conscious that diplomacy these days embraces all kinds of human beings, all types of human experience and behavior.

A great many of the new breed have had military service. These officers are therefore older, more mature, more accustomed to the problems of a large organization than were their predecessors at time of entry. Military service has taught them how to react to dangerous situations and they bring to diplomacy a far better understanding of the military mind. All this brings to the diplomatic establishment a resourcefulness which is essential in these days of cold and hot war.

Those of the new breed who have had military service also bring to the diplomatic establishment an awareness of the preparation required for any serious, professional work. None are more critical than they of the orientation to the diplomatic establishment provided by the Department. They are the ones who demand better educational and training facilities.

The Department will therefore be pushed along the road of improvement by the young officers. But it will be a long time before they reach enough of the strategic strongholds of the Department to do much more than express dissatisfaction. Much that is wrong they see only in fragmentary fashion. They are not experienced enough to trace the deficiencies of the Department back to root causes. They therefore experience difficulty in making sense of much of their dissatisfaction. An interesting innovation of the last few years is a practice of Crockett and the Director General of the Foreign Service to invite younger officers to present their views to them and other senior officers. But the older men cannot always grasp what the younger ones are trying to say. Much of the criticism simply makes no sense to senior officers. Unless they are willing, and have the leisure, to back away from their day-to-day work and study with some detachment the problems which younger officers are pointing out, they will fail to understand the problems no matter how many meetings are held. Since such leisure is rarely available, much of the change which younger men are endeavoring to stimulate can be expected to come slowly.

The process of change could be greatly facilitated by the establishment of an office of basic organizational and personnel research. One of the innovations of the current spurt which has puzzled many people has been the abolition of the Department's office of personnel and the dissipation of its functions among a number of offices and staffs. As a result, effectively coordinated operations are impossible, and there is no longer any possibility for systematic, continuing research into the problems common to all offices of the establishment. This kind of research was, to be sure, never achieved when there was a single "personnel office" for reasons which will have become evident, but now even the opportunity for it is gone.

This situation has aggravated a mystifying phenomenon of the diplomatic establishment: the tendency of each officer to characterize it in a different way. This tendency arises in part from the officers' narrow focus on their daily chores, their future assignments, and their chances for promotion; they conceive of the Department and foreign service in merely subjective terms. But it also stems from the fact that the raw materials for reliable objective views of the Department and foreign service — the raw materials which research could provide — are simply not readily available. Hence, there are almost as many "Departments of State" and "foreign services" as there are officers or types of experiences.

This mystifying variety of images has been reinforced by the kind of orientation officers receive at point of entry into the establishment. At that time, the establishment is not studied, or even described in any depth. Only some of its most talked about, immediately "practical" features are presented, while basic controversial issues are studiously avoided. No one would gather from this orientation that the procedures and problems of the establishment are interrelated or indeed that there *are* serious problems, much less that current features are derivative from basic issues which themselves must be understood if anything about the establishment is to be comprehensible. Hence, orientation seems to say to every incoming officer that there is no need to probe deeply into the Department, the Foreign Service, and their problems, to give them thoughtful and systematic study, to explore the antecedents of current developments and problems. Nor is there any need — orientation seems to say — to compare our diplomatic establishment with those of other governments, so as to gain better perspective and profit from our mistakes and successes. Lacking this fundamental framework within which to fit personal fragments of experience, officers promptly begin to conjure up a "Department of State" and "Foreign Service" in terms of limited and generally superficial impressions. Since important decisions are based upon these illusory images, spurts of improvement introduced by some officers are followed by retrogression by others, progressive moves by reactionary, the process of action and reaction interminably repeated at the cost of consistent evolution. Nothing is more obvious about the Department than that its problems require (1) basic and continuing research so that hard facts may supplant shadowy phantasms, (2) adequate communication of these facts to officers, and (3) enough leisure time for officers so that they can acquaint themselves with these facts. Only in this way can decisions concerning the Department and Foreign Service be based upon data rather than faded lithographs in the minds of older officers and superficial impressions in the minds of the younger.

One must stress the importance not only of hard research and adequate communication, but also of sufficient leisure for officers to keep up with the fruits of research. On this the Secretary has shown himself to be of two minds. Before the Jackson subcommittee he has argued that the Department requires men who can sit back and study long-range issues, knowing very well that only this sort of man can intelligently advise either his own or other governments. But before the Rooney subcommittee, which he knows is interested in saving money, his boast is that notwithstanding the multiplication of independent countries and posts abroad, and of agreements, meetings, responsibilities and crises, he has requested no increase in personnel. Some posts have been cannibalized to staff others. Both in the Department and abroad officers are so hard pressed by the jobs of the moment it is illusory to talk of their thinking of crises which lie in the future, of brooding, of studying. The Secretary has advised the Rooney subcommittee that the increased pressures have been met by "greater individual workloads." They have indeed.

During its current spurt of improvement the Department has not only encouraged an old kind of illiteracy — the failure of men to read and keep abreast of their time — but a new kind caused by the explosion of knowledge during our age — a failure to grasp the implications of new discoveries and breakthroughs so as to synthesize and understand whole areas of new information. Both kinds of illiteracy undermine the kind of foreign policy and diplomacy demanded by a World Power. Preventing the new kind requires more time than coping with the old, for the new areas of information require more study and far more assistance from the best brains of our time. To entrust the training of newly commissioned officers, to the extent the Department does, to ill-read colleagues and bureaucrats and thereafter to swamp and fatigue them on the job, sometimes to the point of collapse, is myopia of the worst kind.

The current spurt of improvement has, in a word, strengthened isolated parts of the Department, but it has also sprayed the old framework of the Department with a paint of rhetoric which, when it peels off some very important places, lays bare a strangely familiar mediocrity.

What is worse, is the fact that the new spurt has failed to provide any fundamental plan with which to coordinate its various improvements, fill in gaps, effect really fundamental change on a broad scale, and assure that its results will have some degree of permanence. When the Kennedy Administration began, the political appointees at the top of the Department gave unmistakable evidence of a belief the Department had "too many people," some of them "not as competent as they should be," and the establishment was "using two people where one competent person should do the job." So the new appointees were really discussing some basic areas of difficulty: the initial selection of officers (were they really as competent as they should be?), training (were officers adequately prepared for their changing and sizable tasks?), the system of promotion (was competence adequately tested and appraised so that the right men were being promoted? did efficiency reports play down inadequate performance in such a way as to make almost impossible eventual separation of inadequate personnel from the Service?), assignments (were these designed to develop the skills the Department needed?), prevailing conditions of service (did these develop or erode the capabilities of officers?). These were basic questions. But in the pressure of world crises upon the summit they were never explored thoroughly. No one had the time.

The Department is in dire need of a general manager who

has the time to explore just these questions, to oversee the establishment in its entirety. It needs a man who can study the relationship between the selection, training and assignment of officers and our foreign policies and diplomacy; who can make sure that the learning and skills which our commitments demand of officers are provided; and who will urge the development and execution of comprehensive plans.

Without this kind of management the weaknesses of the Department are self-perpetuating. For old attitudes are deeply rooted. Old operating procedures are deeply ingrained. Officers who have advanced in rank in a manner satisfactory to themselves see no harm in the excessive rotation they have learned to manipulate to their personal advantage. Officers admitted to the establishment ignorant of international law or the techniques of diplomacy and promoted to the higher echelons see no need of such knowledge. When they sit on examining panels they not only amiably pass the ignorant; they do not even ask such questions in certain areas as might alert successful candidates to their deficiencies. They do not pass on to the training Institute suggestions concerning the gaps which training should fill. In a word, not being professionals, they see no need of professionalization. This is why reformers in the establishment have very hard going. They butt their heads against walls of tradition made firm by the ability of individual officers to take care of themselves.

But if a general manager is to be appointed to level such walls of tradition and thoroughly modernize the establishment, he must be a man experienced in the Department and Foreign Service. He must also be courageously analytical and wise. He must know the ways and objectives of diplomacy so as to keep the Department directed toward one of its primary goals — understanding and influencing people abroad — a task which is overlooked too often in the hectic Washington environment.

For a general manager of the State Department to succeed, Presidents and Secretaries of State must be sophisticated enough to recognize the need for him and to work sympathetically with him. He must continue through Administration changes and be given adequate support for the hard decisions he must make. One President or Secretary must not sidetrack him because he was selected during an earlier Administration. A mere organizational change is not what is needed. What is needed is a sophisticated recognition of the kind of diplomacy our nation requires.

But it is idle to think a Secretary — or a President — will entrust such responsibility to a career officer of the diplomatic establishment until that establishment has won his respect for genuine professionalization and sound operating procedures. The position of general manager would evolve into one of great influence. Much of the establishment's center of gravity would come to settle there. Until the establishment, by preparation and training of officers, earns intellectual and political respect no one is going to give it that much power. This is why orientation, education and training are basic. All thorough reform of the Department comes down to these things. Until the Department gives them the attention they deserve, it will not make substantial and permanent progress toward getting its house in order.

Notes

My BASIC SOURCE of information and interpretation has been of course my study of the diplomatic establishment from the inside. Over the long years of my association with it, I have discussed it and its ways, problems, deficiencies and accomplishments with countless colleagues. The purpose of the following "Notes" is therefore extremely limited. It is to provide (1) sources of quotations and (2) explanatory material which would only encumber the text for the general reader but which offer more detailed and precise commentary to those who wish it. The materials cited, therefore, by no means encompass those which have been consulted over the years.

CHAPTER ONE. DIPLOMACY WENT THATAWAY

page

3 Diplomatic career "parasitical": See Lloyd C. Griscom, *Diplomatically Speaking* (New York: Literary Guild of America, 1940), p. 26, and J. H. Huntington Wilson, *Memoirs of an Ex-Diplomat* (Boston: Bruce Humphries, 1945), p. 45.

Congressman from the Middle West: Champ Clark of Missouri. *Congressional Record*, XLII, 60 Cong., 1 sess. (April 18, 1908), p. 4926. Cited in Warren F. Ilchman, *Professional Diplomacy in the United States, 1779–1939* (Chicago: Univ. of Chicago, 1961), pp. 63–64.

5 "achieved in 1924 as the result of Congressional action": This was the Rogers Act which, in addition to merging the diplomatic and consular corps, provided for a number of improvements in the

newly established Foreign Service. A great measure of the credit
for the Rogers Act and its reforms goes to a civil servant, Wilbur
J. Carr, who, in his forty-five years of service in the Department
devoted himself conscientiously to the improvement of the consular and diplomatic corps, their merger and the betterment of the
resulting Foreign Service. His persistent reform efforts caused such
consternation among the diplomatic officers that he was eventually
sent abroad as Minister to Czechoslovakia. For an authoritative
account of his career, see Katharine Crane's *Mr. Carr of State*
(New York, St. Martin's Press, 1960).

5 The merger of the Department's civil service staff with the Foreign Service was effected upon the basis of *Toward a Stronger
Foreign Service*, Report of the Secretary of State's Public Committee on Personnel (Washington: U. S. Govt. Printing Office,
1954), see note for p. 34. Chairman of the committee was Henry
M. Wriston, president of Brown University, and hence the merger
of the two staffs which ensued in pell-mell fashion became known
as "Wristonization." If the committee missed the profound causes
of the Department's problems and thus placed too great a faith
in the benefits to be expected from merger, it minced no words
in describing the symptoms of the problems — decline in public
confidence in the Department, decline in morale in the diplomatic
establishment, exaggerated emphasis upon generalists in diplomacy, failure to draw fully upon the skills and resources of the
nation, failure to respect Congress's intentions in enacting the
Manpower Act of 1946 (which provided for inducting officers
into all levels of the Foreign Service, so as to make the diplomatic
establishment more flexible and resourceful), etc. The Department's "management of its human resources has been irresolute
and unimaginative," said the committee, even though the question of personnel management "has been under repeated study
since 1945. . . . Substantially nothing has been accomplished"
(pp. 36–37). The committee went on: "All modern personnel
management organizations utilize machines to facilitate the
mechanical tasks of keeping personnel records; the Department
however has not effectively utilized such a system." The Department was accused of "occasional tinkering" with recruitment and
examination of diplomatic officers rather than applying itself
seriously to their improvement. As for the training of officers
through the Foreign Service Institute, the Committee criticized
the Department for a simply "token" recognition of the educational resources of the country. It drew attention to the Congres-

sional desire that the Institute be "for the State Department, what the Naval War College, the Army War College, and the National War College are for the Armed Services — an advanced training ground for officers destined for high command," with the Director of the Institute being "an educational leader of distinction in his field" and his staff including "the best scholars that the universities of the country can furnish." "To this expectation of Congress," said the committee, "substantially no attention has been paid" (p. 45). The committee drew attention to the fact that the Institute's Advisory Committee, which included two Senators and two members of the House of Representatives, had not met for four years. This "revelation" of the Department's "want of energy or interest could scarcely be more dramatic" (p. 47). The committee proceeded: "Here then was an important idea — one for which the pattern had been set in other Government services; one relatively easy of attainment; one which had the support of the Congress and the interest of many citizens across the land. Yet it is dying of neglect. The Department has never developed a clear concept of the training requirements for the officers of the Foreign Service, just as it has never had a program of career planning and development. It has not supplied the Institute with the kind of a Director the Congress stipulated. It has not staffed the Institute with the sort of faculty that was expected. It has not assigned to the Institute students of the grade capable of taking full advantage of the kind of facilities that the Congress intended to supply" (p. 47). All this has a curiously contemporary ring.

6 "These officials had spent years . . .": Along with civil servants who had spent years in the Department working on substantive foreign affairs, Wristonization unfortunately trapped administrative employees of varying grades and functions, such as accountants, who had not been dealing with such affairs but were pressured by the Dulles-Wriston move into the Foreign Service as diplomatic officers. This, of course, was an ill-conceived exaggeration of "merger." For such employees, Wristonization was a cruel hoax.

"The light from the great chandeliers . . .": Griscom, *op. cit.*, pp. 20–21.

8–9 The quotation is from Robert Murphy. *Department of State Bulletin,* December 21, 1959, p. 898. A career Foreign Service officer, Mr. Murphy, following his retirement, published his auto-biography, *Diplomat Among Warriors* (Garden City: Doubleday, 1964).

13 Dean Acheson: Letter to Senator J. William Fulbright, chairman, U. S. Senate Committee on Foreign Relations. Published in *Hearing Before the Subcommittee on National Security Staffing and Operations of the Committee on Government Operations,* U. S. Senate, 88 Cong., 1 sess. (Washington: U. S. Govt. Printing Office, 1964), pp. 378–383, at pp. 379–380.

CHAPTER TWO. WHO RUNS THE STATE DEPARTMENT?

14 President Coolidge: Quoted in Bertram Hulen, *Inside the Department of State* (New York, London: McGraw-Hill, 1939), p. 38.

16 Hull's reaction to Senator Borah's remarks: Julius Pratt, *Cordell Hull* (New York: Cooper Square, 1964), I, p. 315. For Hull's account of the episode, see *The Memoirs of Cordell Hull* (New York: Macmillan, 1948), I, pp. 649–651.

23 The executive secretariat was originally created in 1946 as the "central secretariat." It was renamed and substantially invigorated by Secretary Marshall in June 1947.

"Establishment of the Foreign Service Institute": The Institute had been preceded by various training programs, some more successful than others. Selective language training in the Foreign Service began in 1895 through the assignment of officers as "student interpreters" to the U. S. legations in Persia, Korea, and Siam. In 1902, ten student interpreter positions were created at Peking for Chinese language training. Training in consular responsibilities dates from 1907, when seven newly commissioned consuls were assigned to the Department of State for a 30-day course of instruction. The purpose was "to give novitiates in the [consular] service some practical training in the running of a consular office before sending them to their posts." To provide a measure of training for both consular and diplomatic officers, the Rogers Act of 1924 provided for the establishment of a Foreign Service School, which discharged its responsibilities mainly by the detail of new Foreign Service officers to divisions of the Department for five or more months before their assignment abroad. During the 1930s the School, rechristened the Foreign Service Officers' Training School, provided junior officers with training in consular and commercial work after their two-year probationary tour abroad. Before going abroad, they received but a few days of orientation. During this same decade, a small number of economic and commercial officers were assigned to universities for graduate studies. During World War II, all training was suspended. It was resumed with the establishment of the Foreign Service Institute. William Barnes and John H. Morgan, *The Foreign Service of the United States: Origins, Development, and Functions* (Washington: U. S. Dept. of State, 1961), pp. 156–157, 210–211, 220–221, 262, 285. Ilchman, *op. cit.*, 240. "The Foreign Service Institute: Twenty Years in Retrospect" in *Department of State News Letter*, November 1966, pp. 22 ff.

24 An additional factor of stultification of planning under Secretary Dulles was the low esteem in which the director of planning — an "outsider" — held many of the career diplomatic officers assigned to the planning staff. Although frequently absent for long intervals, the director was considered by his subordinates to delegate little or nothing to his deputy, a career diplomatic officer, so that the staff suffered from lack of work, guidance, and stimulation. More than one member complained that for long periods he was kept "up in the air," not knowing what he was supposed to do.

28 "Bureaucratic termites" and "janitors": A typical expression of this view is to be found in Ellis O. Briggs, *Farewell to Foggy Bottom* (New York: David McKay, 1964). See also his "The Sad State of the Department of State: Part I, The Hog-Tied Ambassador," in *Esquire*, September 1963, pp. 100 ff. Prior to his retirement in 1963, Mr. Briggs was a career Foreign Service officer who rose to the rank of ambassador. Administrative officers Mr. Briggs describes as "administrative types who inflate themselves with all sorts of rich and resonant titles like Career Evaluators, and General Services Specialists, and even Ministers of Embassy for Administrative Affairs. These glorified janitors, supply clerks, and pants-pressers yearn to get their fingers in the foreign affairs pie, and when they do, the diplomatic furniture often gets marked with gummy thumbprints." *Farewell to Foggy Bottom*, p. 29.

CHAPTER THREE. THE SELF-WINDING CLOCK

34 "In 1953 an Under Secretary": This was General Walter Bedell Smith, who discovered to his "horror" that although Congress

had appropriated funds to expand the language training program of the Foreign Service, in response to his "having argued and begged and pleaded and made the most convincing statements I possibly could" for the funds, "there were no Foreign Service officers who could be sent for language training because they could not be spared." *Hearings before a Subcommittee of the Committee on Government Operations*, House of Representatives, 84 Cong., 1 sess. (Washington: U. S. Govt. Printing Office, 1956), p. 609. He conferred with President Eisenhower, wrote a memorandum for Secretary of State Dulles proposing a committee to "get something started" and so a committee came into being headed by Dr. Henry M. Wriston (*ibid.*, p. 608). General Smith also found that the Foreign Service had been so reduced in numbers "there were no Foreign Service officers who could be brought in for key positions in the State Department" (*ibid.*, pp. 609–610), and he was unable to find available officers to fill vacancies in the higher military schools, to which a handful of Foreign Service officers were sent. General Smith got recommendations for the committee's membership from ex-President Herbert Hoover and Philip Young, chairman of the Civil Service Commission (*ibid.*, p. 612).

37 Llewellyn Thompson. More recently, in 1966, this officer was reappointed to a second tour of duty as ambassador to the USSR.

41 Under Secretary's staff meetings: *Task Force Report on Foreign Affairs*, prepared for the Commission on Organization of the Executive Branch of the Government (Washington: U. S. Govt. Printing Office, 1948), p. 78. The Task Force stated: "No planned agenda [for the Under Secretary's staff meetings] exists and most participants are reluctant to bring up matters of real importance. For example, the geographic office directors seem to feel that representatives of the functional units are not to be trusted while the functional representatives often feel that if a problem is raised it may be seized by the geographic offices and settled with the top command via the back door."

CHAPTER FOUR. AT ARM'S LENGTH

46–47 "rival claimants," "a different mission": A classic statement of this point of view will be found in the testimony of Robert A. Lovett before the Senate Subcommittee on National Policy Machinery on February 23, 1960. See *Organizing for National*

Security. *Inquiry of the Subcommittee on National Policy Machinery for the Committee on Government Operations, U. S. Senate* (Washington: Govt. Printing Office, 1961), pp. 12 ff. See also Briggs, *op. cit.*

48 I have borrowed the "old farm" metaphor from *Administrative Management in the Government of the United States.* Report of the President's Committee on Administrative Management (Washington: U. S. Govt. Printing Office, 1937), p. 32.

51 "a quality of Olympian majesty": *Task Force Report on Foreign Affairs,* p. 56.

53 The quoted statement before a Congressional committee: *ibid.,* p. 60.

54 "What Presidential order?": It was not until 1966 that the President "directed the Secretary of State, as his agent, to assume responsibility . . . for the overall direction, coordination and supervision of interdepartmental activities of the United States Government overseas . . ." *Weekly Compilation of Presidential Documents,* vol. 2, no. 9, pp. 317–318.

55 President Truman. *Memoirs by Harry S. Truman,* II (*Years of Trial and Hope*), (Garden City: Doubleday, 1956), p. 56.

55–56 President Truman: *Ibid.,* p. 58.

56 "State should have read the signals": It is interesting to note that the military establishment had been reading the signals for a long time. Again and again, for fifty years, the military had pleaded for just such a body as the National Security Council. See Samuel P. Huntington, *The Soldier and the State: The Theory and Practice of Civil-Military Relations* (Cambridge: Harvard Univ., 1957), p. 263.

60 "a mere curiosity," "form of status seeking," "principal cause for the delays and difficulties": Here, again, the voice is Mr. Lovett's but the attitude has been that of the vast pyramid of the State Department. See *Organizing for National Security,* pp. 12, 15.

61–62 Cordell Hull: *Memoirs,* I, p. 203.

64 "country by country . . . review": In one of its periodic spurts, the State Department had earlier engaged in this sage exercise. This was in late 1946, when crises in Turkish and Greek affairs

confronted the Department with the urgent necessity of analyzing these two countries in depth. The exercise spread to other countries but, so far as I am aware, involved no systematic consultation with other departments and agencies of our government. Like many another spurt, this one died as crises evaporated and the alert minds which had sparked it were rotated to other assignments.

67 "unsystematic inter-agency committees": An exception to such committees was one established at the initiative of President Kennedy in March 1962. The great interest of the President and his staff in Latin America and his commitment to the Alliance for Progress brought to their attention considerable inadequacy in the State Department's handling of affairs. Accordingly, at White House suggestion the Department established a Latin American Policy Committee chaired by the Assistant Secretary of State for Inter-American Affairs and having on it representatives of the President, the Department of Defense (the Joint Chiefs of Staff and the Office of International Security Affairs), USIA, and CIA. Not represented on it were Treasury, Commerce, Labor, and Agriculture to mention only four departments with considerable interest in the problems of this area. The committee met regularly once a week, on a set day. It still exists.

68 The President's announcement: White House press release, March 4, 1966. See note for page 54.

CHAPTER FIVE. THE WORD AND THE SWORD

72 "military, after paddling in the pond of diplomacy": Briggs, *op. cit.*, p. 172.

75 Beaulac's experience is related in his *Career Ambassador* (New York: Macmillan, 1951), p. 103.

79 Marshall: Quoted by Richard W. Leopold, *The Growth of American Foreign Policy: A History* (New York: Alfred A. Knopf, 1962), p. 653.

Senator Vandenburg: quoted *ibid.*, p. 641.

80 "Yugoslavia's defection": This is not to say that the Greco-Bulgarian and Greco-Albanian borders were untroubled after the Yugoslav defection, but only that the Yugoslav defection was crucial.

81 John W. Masland and Laurence I. Radway, *Soldiers and Scholars: Military Education and National Policy* (Princeton: Princeton Univ. 1957), p. 26.

83–84 Murphy's experience is related in his *Diplomat Among Warriors*, pp. 68–70. See also p. 102.

83 State Department's view of political advisers to major military commanders: See "POLAD's Role with the Military," *Department of State News Letter*, No. 31 (November 1963), pp. 7 and 30. See also Memorandum on the Department of State's Political-Military Organization and Staff, printed in *Hearing Before the Subcommittee on National Security Staffing and Operations of the Committee on Government Operations*, U. S. Senate, 88 Cong., 1 sess., Part 6 (December 11, 1963), pp. 413–419.

88 "strong civilian mentality": It will be observed that my interpretation of the development of civilian values and attitudes in the military differs from that of some other writers on the subject. Samuel P. Huntington, for example, is of the opinion that: "As the military acquired authority and influence during the war [World War II], they slowly abandoned their pre-war attitudes and accepted the assumptions and values of civilian thinking." See *The Soldier and the State*, p. 332. The acceptance of "the assumptions and values of civilian thinking" is fairly evident at the turn of the century and might indeed be traceable to the beginnings of our nation.

"a diplomatic officer's 'appreciation' ": For an example of this see Francis T. Underhill, Jr., "Applicability — The Dilemma of Military Power," *Foreign Service Journal*, vol. 42, no. 7 (July 1965), p. 20.

CHAPTER SIX. OF SECRET OPERATIONS AND MUCH CONFUSION

93–96 Yardley's experiences are related in his *The American Black Chamber* (Indianapolis: Bobbs-Merrill, 1931).

98 President Truman: *Task Force Report on Foreign Affairs*, p. 92.

104–105 President Truman's newspaper article, syndicated by the North American Newspaper Alliance, appeared in the *Washington Post* and the *Kansas City Star* on December 22, 1963.

105 Allen W. Dulles, *The Craft of Intelligence* (New York: Harper & Row, 1963), p. 86.

107 Senator Mansfield, *Congressional Record*, vol. 100, 83 Cong., 2 sess. (March 10, 1954), p. 2987.

CHAPTER SEVEN. THE FRONT LINE

117 David Eugene Thompson is described by William Franklin Sands in *Our Jungle Diplomacy* (Chapel Hill: Univ. of North Carolina, 1944), pp. 123 ff.

118–119 Jusserand's relations with President Theodore Roosevelt were so highly personal and intimate that neither of them evidently deemed it prudent to refer to them *in extenso*. Suggestive references may, however, be found in *Letters of Theodore Roosevelt*, selected and edited by Elting E. Morison (Cambridge: Harvard University Press, 1951), volumes IV and V, and in Jusserand's autobiography, *What Me Befell* (Boston: Houghton Mifflin, 1933). Not only by the President but by many private citizens and groups in the United States the French ambassador justly deemed himself "not considered to be really a foreigner" (*What Me Befell*, p. 282). Jusserand says of the period of John Hay's illness and later: "During the brief interval between the cessation of Mr. Hay's functions and the assuming of them by Mr. Root, the President continued to use me as a friendly adviser *amicus curiae*, calling me John Hay. Some time afterwards, as he was discussing confidential matters with a Senator, he thought he noticed a little surprise on his visitor's face at the presence, among a few intimate friends, of the French Ambassador. 'Never mind,' said the President, 'he has taken the oath of Secretary of State.'" *Ibid*, pp. 302–303.

118 Robert Kennedy, *We Must Meet Our Duty and Convince the World That We Are Just Friends and Brave Enemies* (New York: Harper and Row, 1962), p. 24.

120–121 Henry S. Villard, "How to Save Money: An Open Letter to Congressman John J. Rooney," *Harper's* magazine, January 1964, pp. 20–22. The episode is also related in the author's *Affairs at State* (New York: Thomas Y. Crowell, 1965), pp. 196–197. For additional testimony along this line see memorandum on "Impressions of a Recent Ambassadorial Experience," by George F. Kennan, *Hearing before the Subcommittee on National Security Staffing and Operations*, 88 Cong., 1 sess., pp. 358 ff.

121 Earl E. T. Smith, *The Fourth Floor* (New York: Random House, 1962). Ambassador Smith maintains in his book, as in his earlier

testimony before the Subcommittee to Investigate the Administration of the Internal Security Act and Other Internal Security
Laws of the Committee on the Judiciary, U. S. Senate, 86 Cong.,
2 sess. (see *Hearings* of this Subcommittee, Washington: U. S.
Govt. Printing Office, 1960, pp. 681–710) that while he could
talk with officials in the Department higher than the level of
Assistant Secretary, policies were made at that level and below.
His view is that "actions by the lower echelon and those who are
influential in the lower echelon form our policy, and when those
higher up act upon them, the policies have already been determined by events." (*Hearings*, pp. 705–706.) While Secretary
Herter indignantly denied this (Washington *Evening Star*, November 30, 1962), this kind of "layering" problem does exist and
Mr. Herter's successor has candidly conceded it. (See Secretary
Rusk's testimony before the Subcommittee on National Security
Staffing and Operations, 88 Cong., p. 398). Secretary Rusk has
been candid, also, in admitting the difficulty the top echelons
have in considering all questions of importance — "to get time to
think" — and the corresponding reliance of the Department on
the lower echelons. (*Ibid.*, pp. 386–412.) Our discussion in chap-
ters 2 and 3 is relevant to this point.

122 John S. Badeau, "USA and UAR: Crisis in Confidence," *Foreign
Affairs*, vol. 43, No. 2 (January 1965), pp. 281–296.

123–126 Ellis O. Briggs, *Esquire*, pp. 101, 150. The same episode
and views are set forth in the author's *Farewell to Foggy Bottom*,
pp. 168 ff. Many Foreign Service officers feel that Briggs's
attitude is not responsive, either, to the demands made upon an
ambassador's subordinates by the reporting required of them by
the State Department and other parts of the Federal Government. Economic reporting is in itself a major demand. Subordinates who do not meet these demands are subject to adverse
ratings by Department officers, affecting their subsequent assignments and chances of promotion. An ambassador can take a
lordly attitude toward staff reductions but if these are not related
to required responsibilities his staff can be victimized and its
morale seriously affected. Much loose talk is bandied about in the
establishment about "overstaffing." An interesting experience is
that of George F. Kennan, a career diplomatic officer who at one
time in his career talked in this vein, but when appointed ambassador to Yugoslavia in 1961 could not suggest reductions in his large
staff. His candid confession was set forth in his memorandum on
"Impressions of a Recent Ambassadorial Experience."

CHAPTER EIGHT. OF GULLIVER IN LILLIPUT

130 "rarely well informed": Even when informed, as Herbert Hoover
was by virtue of his earlier Cabinet position, he may have acquired
unfavorable impressions of the diplomatic establishment. Not
only did he find there were "poor relations between the State and
Commerce departments over their foreign services" when he became Secretary of Commerce in 1921, but, more important, State
had failed to keep in modern repair our commercial treaties.
These were outdated. Some were a century old. At Hoover's
initiative, a joint committee of Commerce and State was created
to bring about their revision. *The Memoirs of Herbert Hoover.
The Cabinet and the Presidency, 1920–1933* (New York: Macmillan, 1952), p. 37.

133 "president of a department store chain": This individual was
Maxwell H. Gluck, designated as ambassador to Ceylon in 1957.
Many career officers have gleefully seized upon this example as
illustrative of the kind of people Presidents appoint as ambassadors when they go outside the career ranks. What they do not
understand is that Presidents view *them* as partly responsible for
humiliations like this. Following the Gluck affair, the pyramidal
mass of the Department was instructed to brief Presidential appointees *prior to* their appearance before the Senate Committee
on Foreign Relations, not *after*, as had been the practice. The
condemnation by career officers of such fiascos as the Gluck one
has therefore missed an important point in the minds of Presidents.

138 Dean Acheson, "The President and the Secretary of State," in
The Secretary of State, Don K. Price, ed. (Englewood Cliffs, N.J.:
Prentice-Hall, 1960), p. 45. An extended treatment of this prob-
lem is provided by Louis W. Koenig in *The Invisible Presidency*
(New York: Rinehart, 1960).

139 This incident and its consequences are described at length by
Mr. Morrison in his *Latin American Mission* (New York: Simon
& Schuster, 1965), pp. 100 ff.

142 Harry Hopkins: By 1944 the enormity of the chasm between the
White House and the State Department had begun to impress
even so great a contributor to and exploiter of it as Hopkins.
Having encountered at the first Cairo Conference (1943) a career
Foreign Service officer then stationed in Moscow, plied him with

"all manner of questions about the Soviet Union," and been "impressed by the objectivity and lack of bias as well as by the considerable scholarship revealed in his answers," Hopkins subsequently arranged for this officer to be assigned to the White House as a liaison officer with the State Department. See Robert E. Sherwood, *Roosevelt and Hopkins: An Intimate History* (New York: Harper & Brothers, rev. ed. 1950), pp. 774–775. The officer was Charles E. Bohlen. By the time this action was taken, Edward R. Stettinius was Secretary of State and the initiative of taking this step is attributed to him by Richard L. Walker in his biographical essay on Stettinius which is combined with George Curry's on James F. Byrnes to form vol. XIV of *The American Secretaries of State and Their Diplomacy* (New York: Cooper Square, 1965), p. 24. Walker bases this attribution upon Stettinius' own record in his *Roosevelt and the Russians* (Garden City: Doubleday, 1949), p. 12, and William D. Leahy, *I Was There: The Personal Story of the Chief of Staff to Presidents Roosevelt and Truman Based on His Notes Made at the Time* (New York: Whittlesey House, 1950), pp. 280–281. Bohlen's own recollection agrees with the Sherwood account. See extract of his letter to me, dated July 20, 1966, below.

As for the experiment itself, it failed to achieve the broad objective which was sought due to Bohlen's prolonged absences from Washington. It has never been tried again so far as I am aware. Ambassador Bohlen has written me as follows concerning this episode:

"From his experiences at the Conferences of Tehran and Cairo in 1943, Harry Hopkins had come to the conclusion that the White House had a genuine need for some Departmental Liaison Officer who could keep the President, himself, and Admiral Leahy up to date on international events as received in the Department of State, and who would be in a position to obtain quickly for the White House a Departmental recommendation on any given subject.

"At the time of the appointment of Mr. Stettinius, I recall that Mr. Hopkins called me over to the White House and told me he had recommended and the President had accepted my name for this position. I imagine it had also been cleared with Secretary Stettinius, and then the matter went into the machinery and I was formally designated . . . as Assistant to the Secretary of State and White House Liaison Officer. The Sherwood report is correct that Hopkins did arrange for my appointment to this job and the State Department was merely the formal implementation of this decision.

"As to the functions, they were of necessity rather loose. I used to go over to the White House every day and consult with Hopkins, Admiral Leahy, and very often President Roosevelt. I would also bring back to the Secretary of State, or the appropriate officer in the Department, matters which required decision. I should mention that I only held this position from about the middle of December 1944 until immediately after Roosevelt's death April 12, 1945. Following Roosevelt's death, and the subsequent appointment of Jimmy Byrnes as Secretary of State, the position was dropped, primarily because Mr. Byrnes I believe wished to be his own liaison with President Truman.

"Insofar as I am aware, I was the first and indeed the only Foreign Service officer who was actually appointed as Liaison Officer with the White House. . . . I should add that during this period I was away a good deal, having left with Mr. Hopkins to go to London prior to the Yalta Conference, from which we returned about the middle of March. I was then in San Francisco from about April 25 until the end of May, when I went to Moscow with Hopkins, returning to San Francisco to work on the Russian Language Panel, and from there practically immediately to Potsdam."

143–146 Theodore Roosevelt's diplomacy is well described in Sidney Warren, *The President as World Leader* (Philadelphia: J. B. Lippincott, 1964), pp. 36–45.

147–148 Clinton Rossiter, *The American Presidency* (New York: Harcourt, Brace, 1956), p. 25.

149 "the man credited with that deeply resented occupation": This was Josephus Daniels, Secretary of the Navy at the time of the Vera Cruz incident. When appointed ambassador to Mexico, Mr. Daniels even proposed to enter Mexico by way of Vera Cruz, as he and his wife enjoyed traveling by ship. When dissuaded by the State Department from this folly, he traveled by train, the Mexican Government deeming it prudent to take special police and even military precautions to protect him from anticipated demonstrations from the border to Mexico City. More than 350 police were reported by Daniels to have been present at the railroad station in Mexico City alone, when he arrived. He adds:

"Half a dozen blocks from the station to the Embassy had been blocked off with police and a large guard was on duty at the Embassy." This extraordinary affair is related in Mr. Daniels's *Shirt-Sleeve Diplomat* (Chapel Hill: Univ. of North Carolina, 1947), pp. 1–14.

CHAPTER NINE. DIFFERENT WORLDS

154 Assistant Secretary of State for Congressional Relations: Frederick G. Dutton. *Department of State News Letter*, No. 16 (August 1962), p. 18.

156–157 The quotation is from Lester Markel, Hanson W. Baldwin and others, *Public Opinion and Foreign Policy* (New York: Harper, 1949), p. 24. See also p. 90.

158 The long-time member of Congress quoted is Senator Karl E. Mundt. See *Organizing for National Security*, p. 1299. Congressman John Brademas once told a newly-commissioned group of diplomatic officers that "the heat that Congress turns on them originates from their constituents, and cited one of the Congressman's chief tasks as being 'how to vote in the national interest and get away with it.' " He advised officers they "could help him and his colleagues 'get away with it' by being sensitive to their informational needs." Winston Lord, "FSO–8 Lectured on Congressional Relations," *Department of State News Letter*, No. 16 (August 1962), p. 21.

160–161 The Department civil servant dismissed is, of course, Otto F. Otepka, and the diplomatic officer, William Wieland. The Congressional and other public documentation of this "blaze" is considerable. It includes hearings before the Subcommittee to Investigate the Administration of the Internal Security Act and other Internal Security Laws of the Committee on the Judiciary, U. S. Senate, 87 Congress (1961–1962) and 88 Congress (1963–1964). During the 89 Congress the Subcommittee gave further consideration to the controversy. The press has given considerable space to it. Charles Stevenson summarized the information at his disposal in "The Ordeal of Otto Otepka," *Reader's Digest*, (August 1965), pp. 55–59. Besides Otepka, the controversy cost two other State Department officials their careers. The smoldering embers periodically break into flame.

168 Briggs: *Esquire*, p. 101.

170 "a practice which ought to be stopped": see, for instance, Legislative Report 3795, dated for release March 17, 1965, of Congressman H. R. Gross. The view was repeated in the Congressman's Legislative Report 884, dated for release November 30, 1966.

172–173 *Hearings before a Subcommittee of the Committee on Appropriations*, House of Representatives, 88 Cong., 2 sess., "Department of State" (Washington: U. S. Govt. Printing Office, 1965), p. 335.

174 Quotation from testimony of Thomas L. Hughes, Director of Intelligence and Research, Department of State, in *Hearings before a Subcommittee of the Committee on Appropriations*, House of Representatives, 89 Cong., 1 sess., "Department of State" (Washington: U. S. Govt. Printing Office, 1965), p. 335.

175–176 Cordell Hull: *Memoirs*, p. 183.

178–179 *Hearings before a Subcommittee of the Committee on Appropriations*, House of Representatives, 88 Cong., 2 sess., p. 39.

180–181 McCleod: Characterization of young officers as "babies" was made orally before incoming classes at the Foreign Service Institute. McLeod's Congressional testimony will be found in *Hearings before the Subcommittee to Investigate the Administration of the Internal Security Act*, etc., 87 Cong., pp. 433 ff.

181 The State Department, it appears, does not invariably favor the appointment of Congressmen to delegations to international conferences. DeLesseps Morrison for example, reports "a State Department recommendation that no Congressman should be included in our delegation to Punta del Este," the Inter-American conference of 1961. *Latin American Mission*, p. 167.

CHAPTER TEN. ON WINNING FRIENDS AND INFLUENCING PEOPLE

187–188 Quotation from Lester Markel, *op. cit.*, p. 136. The burden on diplomatic officers has been somewhat relieved by the appointment of public affairs officers to each bureau.

193 "increasing criticism from the elite public": Several former Department officers helped to introduce this period of criticism, including Joseph M. Jones, who published A *Modern Foreign Policy for the United States* in 1944, and Bryton Barron, *Inside the State Department* in 1956. These were followed by the American

Assembly's *The Secretary of State* in 1960, in which former Department officials, including Dean Acheson, collaborated with scholars in measured criticism. On the part of career diplomatic officers, Willard Beaulac contributed informative candor and Ellis O. Briggs vehement criticism in *Career Ambassador* (1951) and *Farewell to Foggy Bottom* (1964) respectively, while ambassadors of political appointment have delivered such ungloved criticism as Stanton Griffis' *Lying in State* (1952) and Earl E. T. Smith's *Fourth Floor* (1962).

From outside the establishment have come Robert Bendiner's stinging *Riddle of the State Department* (1942), *Public Opinion and Foreign Policy* by Lester Markell and others (1949), and James S. Childer's *The Nation on the Flying Trapeze* (1960), along with numerous articles, editorials, Letters to the Editor, and the best-selling of all, that factual critique in the guise of a novel, *The Ugly American* (1958).

Scholars have been more cautious, lacking suitable materials and experience, but have been casting increasingly critical asides in their works, as in Thomas A. Bailey's *The Man in the Street* (1948), Oskar Morgenstern's *The Question of National Defense* (1959), Edwin O. Reischauer's *Wanted: An Asian Policy* (1955), and Elmer Plischke's *Conduct of American Foreign Policy* (1961). Direct criticism has occurred in several studies of the Brookings Institution, including that undertaken in 1950 at the request of the Bureau of the Budget, *The Administration of Foreign Affairs and Overseas Operations* (Washington: Brookings Institution, 1951), James L. McCamy's *Administration of American Foreign Affairs* (1950), and *Conduct of the New Diplomacy* (1964), Zara Steiner's two studies on *The State Department and the Foreign Service* (1958) and *Present Problems of the Foreign Service* (1961). When scholars have had experience in international affairs, as Michael H. Cardozo and Arthur M. Schlesinger, Jr., they have produced critical *Diplomats in International Cooperation* (1962) and *A Thousand Days* (1965) respectively. In addition to writing books, various authors have lectured extensively.

197–199 James S. Childers, *The Nation on the Flying Trapeze* (New York: D. McKay, 1960), pp. 5–6, 274–276.

CHAPTER ELEVEN. THE CURRENT SPURT

208 Assistant Secretary for Far Eastern Affairs: The title of this bureau was changed in November 1966 to East Asian and Pacific Affairs.

209 Although Secretary Rusk came into office critical of the amount of traveling his predecessor had done, it took Dulles some six years (1953–1959) to establish a record 559,988 miles and Rusk less than five to exceed this with 587,913. By mid-1966, Mr. Rusk had also traveled twice as much within the United States as Mr. Dulles — 160,868 miles to 80,702. *Department of State News Letter*, July 1966, p. 29.

216 "overwhelmed with work": Quotation from ex-Secretary of State James F. Byrnes, "Stop Shooting Our Sentries!" *Collier's*, November 11, 1955.

218 "These seminars, for lack of funds": As a matter of fact, few, if any, funds for these were available from Congressional appropriations. Our ambassador to Ireland, Raymond R. Guest, a political appointee, donated his salary for the purpose. Private funds had to be sought also for a pilot seminar on science in the Foreign Service Institute.

219 "well-researched consideration": Ten years earlier, in one of its spurts of improvement, the Department had established a small planning staff in the Office of Personnel, but it was quietly abolished in 1953, "to vanish without a trace," as the Wriston Committee reported. See *Toward a Stronger Foreign Service*, pp. 36–37. After the abolition of the Office of Personnel by Crockett, an Office of Management Planning picked up a part of the slack in needed personnel and management research, but made slow headway in gaining support for its recommendations due to the resistance of the pyramidal mass. When this office was, in turn, abolished in 1966, the Department became reduced to a good deal of dispersed tinkering with personnel and management problems.

222 "one official felt so strongly": The reference, again, is to the Otepka-Wieland affair. See note for pages 160–161.

222–223 American Legion: *Report on the U. S. Department of State by the American Legion Special Liaison Committee* (Indianapolis, 1964).

226 attitudes toward training: See John H. Stutesman, "A New Mid-Level Training Program," *Department of State News Letter*, No. 58 (February 1966), pp. 21, 51.

228 Arthur M. Schlesinger, Jr., *A Thousand Days* (Boston: Houghton Mifflin, 1965), p. 407.

229–230 public advisory groups: The Department's announcement of "plans for the creation of several panels of civilian specialists from outside government to serve as advisers to the Department on a broad range of foreign policy matters" was made in its press release No. 246, October 18, 1966. *Department of State Bulletin,* Vol. LV, No. 1428 (November 7, 1966), pp. 721–722. The panel was announced at that time for the Bureau of International Organization Affairs. Three weeks later, the Department announced its panel for the Bureau of East Asian and Pacific Affairs. Press Release No. 270, November 10, 1966. As of this writing (in early December 1966) panels have not been announced for the Bureaus of European Affairs and Near East and South Asian Affairs nor for the Policy Planning Council. The Advisory Council on African Affairs was announced on June 11, 1962 and met promptly on June 13–14. See the Department's press release No. 384 of June 11, 1962, briefly summarized in *Department of State Bulletin,* Vol. XLVII, No. 1201 (July 2, 1962), pp. 24–25. It is interesting to note that the Department of Commerce established its advisory committee on "policies and undertakings of the Department" in 1921. The *Memoirs of Herbert Hoover,* p. 41.

230 The 1946–53 advisory committee was an interesting example of a long-sustained improvement made possible by non-rotating civil servants, particularly an outstanding officer of the Department, Joseph C. Green, who fell a casualty of McCarthyism. Mr. Green was the author of the letter from which a passage dealing with the termination of this committee was printed by the Senate Foreign Relations Committee. *Study of United States Foreign Policy: Summary of Views of Retired Foreign Service Officers.* Prepared for the Committee on Foreign Relations, United States Senate, pursuant to the provisions of S. Res. 31, 86 Cong. 1 sess. (Washington: U. S. Govt. Printing Office, 1959), p. 48.

CHAPTER TWELVE. BY WAY OF CONCLUSION

237 "Those of career status, like Crockett . . .": On January 18, 1966, came the announcement of Crockett's resignation from the government, the reasons for which were not clear.

239 The phrases quoted are from a progenitor of the New Breed, Arthur C. Millspaugh, an American financial and economic adviser to the Iranian Government in 1922 and again in 1944. See his *Americans In Persia* (Washington: Brookings Institution, 1946), p. 208.

240 "living in different worlds": A characteristic of the new breed is its desire to be involved in the formulation of foreign policy. While the diplomatic establishment continues to attract people interested in prestige and status, it attracts a sizable proportion who have a serious interest in policy making. Since they do not understand diplomacy, however, they have no conception of the bits and pieces which must be put together abroad, by both consular posts and embassies, in order to make policy effective. They are not aware of the extent to which these "bits and pieces" in fact influence policy and indeed *make* policy. They therefore become bored with the "bits and pieces," creating a very serious morale problem in the Service. They share the psychology of many young people of wanting to get ahead fast, do "big" things and make "big" decisions early in their careers. They do not always reflect that as representatives of a nation they require a good deal of seasoning experience for this kind of thing.

245–246 "strengthened isolated parts": I do not share the exuberant appraisal of progress made to date and prospects for further advances in the Department's renovation expressed by Alfred J. Marrow in his "Managerial Revolution in the State Department," *Personnel*, vol. 43, no. 6 (November–December 1966), pp. 8–18. Mr. Marrow is chairman of the board of Harwood Mfg. Corp. and a consultant to the Department. His enthusiasm suggests that he is unaware of how deeply rooted are the prevailing attitudes and procedures of the diplomatic establishment. A promising attack on attitudes has been made by Crockett through "management seminars" in which the resources of psychologists are used for "sensitivity training." Lack of adequate funds, however, is restricting this program to such a degree that the "revolution" it promises will be very slow in coming.

246 "political appointees . . . gave unmistakable evidence": Alfred Puhan, "An Executive Director Writes of Belt-Tightening Plans," *Department of State News Letter*, No. 9 (January 1962), p. 6. Mr. Puhan is a career officer who entered the foreign service via the Office of War Information and the Department of State. In 1962, he was executive director of the Bureau of European Affairs.

INDEX

Index

The notes referred to in this index will be found between pages 249 and 268.